MASCOT ON A MISSION

DAN MEERS

FOREWORD BY BOBBY BELL

MASCOT ON A MISSION

Copyright © 2023 Cross Training Publishing

ISBN 978-1-938254-94-9

MASCOT ON A MISSION / Dan Meers
Published by Cross Training Publishing,
Omaha, Nebraska 68137

Distributed in the United States and Canada by Cross Training Publishing

Unless otherwise indicated, all Scripture quotations are from the *Holy Bible, New International Version,* © 1973, 1978, 1984, International Bible Society. Used by permission of Zondervan Bible Publishers. Other quotations are taken from *New American Standard Bible,* (NASB) © The Lockman Foundation 1960, 1962, 1963, 1968, 1971, 1972, 1973, 1975, 1977, the *Revised Standard Version of the Bible* (RSV) © 1946, 1952, 1971, 1973, the *Authorized/King James Version* (KJV).

Contents

CROSS TRAINING

For additional books and resources available
through Cross Training Publishing contact us at:

Cross Training Publishing
15418 Weir Street #177
Omaha, NE 68137
(308) 293-3891
www.crosstrainingpublishing.com

For more information on Dan Meers, Rod Handley and
Character that Counts contact us at:

Character That Counts
512 N.E. Victoria Drive
Lee's Summit, MO 64086
www.characterthatcounts.org

Preface

For more than 30 years I have gone to work in a costume. I run around dressed as KC Wolf, with 85 inch hips and 23 inch tennis shoes. I like to think of myself as Kansas City's biggest party animal. As a mascot, I spend my time wearing a mask and pretending to be something I'm not. As a man, my goal is much different. My goal as a man is to be real. I want to be authentic. When I think back on my life the people who had the greatest influence on me were not the ones who were trying to impress me. No, the people who have the greatest influence on my life are those who are genuine and real. They live authentic lives. My prayer as I write this book is it will somehow have a positive influence and impact on your life.

My goal is not to impress you. When you get to my age you really don't worry too much about what others think. My goal as a man and as an author is strictly to be real. My life is a lot like yours–filled with the good, the bad and the ugly. As you read this book, please keep in mind it is written by an imperfect man with issues. Life is hard. We all have issues we struggle with in this life. I'm no different. My wife is a counselor, and she likes to say it's the people who don't think they have issues who really have issues. The good news is God still uses people like you and me who have issues to make this world a better place to live.

In the back of my Bible I have written this quote, "God didn't put us on earth to make a living, He put us here to make an impact." This book is filled with stories of people I've met on my mascot journey who are difference makers. People who have had an impact on my life. They're not perfect people, but they are individuals using their lives to positively influence and impact those around them. I pray this book and the stories in it will encourage and challenge you to be intentional and look for ways to make a positive impact in your home, workplace and community. Together I believe we can make our world a better place to live.

I might be a 56-year-old man who has issues, bad eyes and a small bladder but I'm also a "Mascot on a Mission" trying to have a positive impact in the lives of others. Thank you so much for taking time to read my book. I hope it brings joy to your day, puts a smile on your face, and encourages you to become more mission minded.

Foreword by Bobby Bell

During my 11 years playing linebacker and defensive end in the National Football League, I had the opportunity to meet many exceptional people. Some were loud and boisterous and loved to entertain, while others were quiet and shied away from the limelight. My good friend Dan Meers was an interesting combination of both. Although people may not immediately recognize his name, Dan has been one of the biggest entertainers at Kansas City Chiefs games for more than 30 years. The reason you never hear his name called on game day or see his face on the Jumbotron is because Dan works undercover. Specifically, he works under the cover of fur. You see Dan is better known as KC Wolf, the official mascot of the Kansas City Chiefs.

I first met Dan when he started working for the Chiefs back in 1990. What made Dan so unique was he literally had two personalities he switched on and off. For most people, having multiple personalities is not a positive trait, but in Dan's case he turned it into something amazing. On game day, while dressed up as KC Wolf he acted like a wild man who loved being out in front of the crowd entertaining the fans. However, once the game ended and the costume came off, Dan was one of the most laid-back and mild-mannered guys I had ever met. Whenever you'd see Dan out of costume you would never guess his alter ego was the Kansas City Chiefs' biggest party animal.

Dan and I got to know each other better through numerous appearances at Chiefs functions and other community events. Although I played as an NFL linebacker and defensive end, and Dan performed as an NFL mascot, one of the things we had in common was our love of Kansas City. Since we both spent our careers working for the Chiefs, we grew to love the city and our beloved Chiefs fans.

Over the years, I watched Dan develop KC Wolf into much more than just another sports mascot. What I came to admire most about Dan was he was not only a great mascot, but more importantly he was a genuinely nice guy. He always wore a big smile on his face and made time for others. He didn't just talk about supporting good causes in Kansas City, he actually went out and got involved. Even though his official title at Arrowhead was 'Director of Shenanigans,' Dan's ultimate goal was for KC Wolf to be known as a character with character who was making an impact throughout Chiefs Kingdom and beyond.

Dan is a man who lives his life by design and not default. He doesn't just sit back and watch life happen, but instead he is intentional about using his time, talents and platform to make a positive impact in the lives of others. I'm thankful to call him my friend, and I hope this book will encourage and inspire you to also go out and make a positive impact in your world. Dan Meers is a good example for each of us. He truly is a mascot on a mission, living a life of influence, and because of that Kansas City and this world is a better place.

1

Old Mascots Never Die, They Just Smell Like It

"What counts in life is not the mere fact that we have lived. It is what difference we have made to the lives of others that will determine the significance of the life we lead." - Nelson Mandela

After I finished writing my first book *Wolves Can't Fly* in November 2014, I swore to never write another. Writing a book is tedious work, requiring much time and focus. I definitely don't have a lot of spare time on my hands, and trying to get a mascot to focus is like trying to get a dog to sit still in a room full of squirrels. Some people actually enjoy the challenge of sitting down, framing their thoughts and writing a book, but unfortunately that's not me. I enjoy spending time in front of my computer and writing about as much as I enjoy painting my house.

Although writing a book is hard work, there are a few benefits. The best part is people think you're smarter than you really are. In school the smart students graduate Magna Cum Laude; I graduated Thank the Laude. If it wasn't for the Good Lord I doubt I would have made it out of school. What's interesting to me is I have been doing public speaking since 1990, and until I became an author most of the speaking requests I received were for small groups close to home. After *Wolves Can't Fly* was published, I went from just being a 'speaker' to being an 'author and speaker.' Apparently, this somehow gave me more credibility because I now get requests to speak to a wide variety of large audiences all over the country. If you ask my brothers, they will be the first to tell you I'm not really any smarter than I was before I wrote a book; I just have a lot more people fooled into thinking I am. I'm hoping now that I've written two books people will think I'm twice as smart.

Another benefit of writing a book is it helps me record and remember many of the great people I've met and the wonderful life experiences I've enjoyed. This book reminds me I am a blessed man. Sure, there are people who make a lot more money than I do. Regardless of what you might think, NFL mascots are no threat to the salary cap. Mascots sweat just as much, and if not more, than NFL players, but the players still get paid significantly more. As I grow older though, I've learned true wealth is measured more by memories than by money, and in that regard I'm a wealthy man. Every time my wife sends me to the grocery store I make a list so I won't forget something. This book is like my grocery list. It's my way of writing things down so I don't forget how blessed I've been during my life journey.

I've also become a lot more comfortable in my own skin. As I get older, I'm not nearly as concerned with what other people think about me. I think part of the reason I didn't really enjoy writing my first book is because I was way too concerned with trying to sound intelligent. I have a new strategy writing this book. I'm not worried with trying to sound intelligent; my main goal is to have more fun. I always like books with lots of pictures and interesting stories that make me laugh, and most importantly make my heart happy. This is what I've been trying to accomplish while writing. My prayer as you read it is for you to be entertained, encouraged and also challenged to go out and make a positive impact in *your* little corner of this world.

Helen Keller once said, "Life is either a daring adventure or nothing at all." I couldn't agree more. I'm not here to just endure life. I need adventure. As long as I'm on this earth I want to take some chances. I want to fill my days with laughter and enjoy this life to the fullest.

Although this book is for people of all ages, I specifically tried to design it to appeal to people my age or older. After turning 50, while I'm still a kid at heart and love to run around at football games acting crazy, I've noticed several things:

1) Ibuprofen is my friend. My brain tells me I'm a young man, which encourages me to do crazy things like sky diving. My body often reminds me that my brain is wrong.

2) My eyes don't work as well as they used to. I now have to wear glasses when I read.

3) My bladder seems to have shrunk to about half of its original size. I can no longer eat watermelon after 7:00 p.m. or I will be up all night going to the bathroom.

4) And while I hate to admit it, I have less energy. Unfortunately I'm now at a point in my life where I can drink a 5 Hour energy drink and it only gives me two hours' worth of energy.

While I enjoy being a kid at heart, I still get plenty of reminders that I'm also now an adult. This was never more apparent than when I went in for my annual health checkup after turning 50. I left my appointment both encouraged and anxious. I was encouraged because after my examination the doctor told me everything looked great. I was the proper weight, and he was happy with both my blood pressure and cholesterol levels. What made me anxious was he also informed me that since I was now 50 years old it was time to get my first COLONOSCOPY. Ugggggghhhh! Not the dreaded COLONOSCOPY!

Since many of my friends had also recently turned 50, I had heard many stories about prepping for the colonoscopy, none of which were pleasant. With much trepidation and fear I called the gastroenterologist (aka butt doctor), and they scheduled my colonoscopy for the following week. The day before the procedure I began the prep. I didn't eat any solid foods and tried to stay hydrated by drinking lots of water and clear liquids. Living on a liquid diet when you already have a small bladder makes for a very unproductive day. Most of my day was spent running back and forth to the men's room. Little did I realize that later that evening, after drinking the special colonoscopy juice, I would spend most of my night camped out in the bathroom.

The instructions in my prep kit said I was supposed to start drinking the special juice at 6:00 p.m. Unfortunately, my last KC Wolf appearance was scheduled from 5:30–6:30 p.m. at the YMCA in Brookfield, MO, which is 125 miles from my home in Kansas City. Although I've never had any formal training as a doctor, I made the decision to postpone drinking the special juice until after my appearance. The thought of getting stuck in my KC Wolf costume after drinking a very strong laxative didn't sound like a good idea, so I waited to begin until 7:00 p.m.

While that was a good choice, my trip back to Kansas City was still one I will never forget. I drank my first bottle of juice, along with three bottles of water, somewhere between Brookfield and Cameron, MO on Highway 36. As I turned onto Interstate 35-South in Cameron and started toward Kansas City, I started to feel rumblings. The special thunder and lightning prep juice was quickly brewing up a powerful storm somewhere deep within my colon. I could tell it was a fast approaching storm. Unfortunately for me, I was still 63 miles away from my house. I won't go into all of the gory details, but suffice it to say it took me a long time to get home because of several emergency stops along the route. When I finally arrived home, I didn't stop to give my wife her usual kiss on my way in the door because I was racing to get to the bathroom.

As much as I don't like getting older, it sure beats the alternative. On my 50th birthday I did a little research and I read a sobering statistic which caused me to stop and reflect on my life. Americans who live to 100 years old comprise just 0.0173 percent of the population. Now I'm no mathematical genius, but even I'm smart enough to understand my chances of making it to age 100 are not very good. The fact I'm a male makes my odds of becoming a centurion even worse. Females almost always live longer than males.

Genealogy in Time Magazine reported the oldest human to ever live (one whose date of birth can be fully documented) was Jeanne Louise Calment from Arles, France. She died in 1997 at the ripe old age of 122 years, 166 days. In many ways, she was remarkable. She is the only person to have ever been confirmed beyond a doubt to have reached the age of 120 years.

An interesting question is how Jeanne Louise Calment managed to achieve such an advanced age. Her friends and family reported she smoked until the age of 117 and ate a couple pounds of chocolate a week. She also rode her bike until the age of 100 and lived on her own until 110. Go figure. Now I'm not saying I want to live to be 120 years old like Jeanne Louise Calment, but I would like to enjoy a long, healthy and meaningful life.

The statistics remind me I'm now at a point where I probably have more sidewalk behind me than in front of me. If my life is a football game, halftime is over. I'm competing in the second half. Some people might look at those statistics and get depressed. Not me. Hearing them just fuels my fire and gives me a sense of urgency. Those statistics remind me I've got a limited number of days on this earth. I want to make the most of the days I'm given. I want my days to count. I want to be intentional and use my days to make an impact in the lives of those around me.

Age has a way of making a person slow down and reflect on life. Saint Augustine once said that asking yourself the question of your own legacy "For what do I want to be remembered?" is the beginning of adulthood. Apparently I am becoming an adult because I've spent a lot of time lately thinking about what kind of legacy I'm leaving. After a lot of thought I've identified a few goals.

One day when my life story comes to a close and people are standing around at my funeral telling stories and reflecting on my life, I want it to be a celebration of a life lived well. I'm not concerned with whether people remember I was the Kansas City Chiefs mascot for more than 30 years or be impressed I was inducted into the Mascot Hall of Fame. I don't really care whether people remember my accomplishments or the awards I've won. When my life story is complete I hope to be remembered for who I was and not for what I did. I hope to be remembered for three things:

1) Most importantly, as a man who loved the Lord with all his heart, soul, mind and strength (Luke 10:27).

2) As a man who loved and adored his family.

3) As a man who loved others and used his time, talent and treasure to make a positive impact in this world.

This is how I hope to be remembered. Jackie Robinson, who was the first African American to play in Major League Baseball, once said, "A life isn't significant except for its impact on other lives." I agree. I've discovered during my career as a mascot that true significance and meaning in life come when I take my eyes off myself and look for opportunities to positively impact others. I believe one reason so many people in our world today walk around discouraged, depressed and feeling like their life isn't making an impact is because they spend the majority of their time and energy chasing worldly success instead of striving for a life of significance.

Let me encourage you to pause and reflect on your own life. What kind of legacy do you want to leave? How do you want to be remembered when your life story is complete? I can tell you that on the day of your funeral it's not going to matter how successful you were. It won't matter how big your house was or how nice a car you drove. You don't get to take either one with you. The only thing which will matter when your life story is complete is your relationships. Most importantly, your relationship with the Lord but also your relationships with those your life has impacted. Former Dallas Cowboys coach Tom Landry said it well, "Everyone is a role model for someone." I think we should strive to be good ones.

For me, I've learned when I make my vertical relationship with the Lord and my horizontal relationships with others the top priorities in my life, then (and only then) am I able to enjoy this life to the fullest. That's when my life has significance and meaning. This is when I'm able to have a positive influence on those around me. Let me challenge you to make your relationships your priority. You will discover just how rewarding life can be.

I hope reading this book will encourage you to live a life of influence. I was taught growing up that your life is like your finances; you can do one of two things. You can spend it, or you can invest it. Money you spend you never see again. Money you invest wisely will multiply and return to you. We do the exact same thing with our lives. We choose to spend it or we choose to invest it. A life spent selfishly is wasted, but a life invested in impacting and influencing others will bear fruit for an eternity.

I have a passion for encouraging others to live as investors, not only with their money but more importantly with their lives. Over the course of my lifetime I have had hundreds of people who invested in me and impacted who I am today. Some people, like my parents, have been a constant encouragement and influence since the day I was born. Others had an impact for a short season of my life. Still others have been folks God brought into my life for a brief moment, but they still left a lasting impression. The common denominator with these people is they chose to live as investors. They made deposits into my life, and I am forever grateful. In the chapters ahead I want to share stories of some of the people I've met during my mascot career and the character qualities that made them difference makers in this world. My prayer is these stories will entertain, encourage and inspire you to have a positive impact and influence.

American cartoonist Scott Adams once said, "You don't have to be a 'person of influence' to be influential. In fact some of the most influential people in my life are probably not even aware of the things they've taught me." His quote reminds me that each and every one of us has the power to influence the lives of those around us.

Regardless of age, economic status or position in life, each of us has the ability to positively impact our world. Over the course of my mascot career I've discovered when I choose to live a life of influence, focused on others, it not only enriches the lives of those around me but it enriches my own life as well. If you don't believe me I encourage you to try it, but be careful, it might just change your life.

Becoming Mission Minded: What kind of life story are you writing? What would you like people to say about you at your funeral? How can you become more intentional to ensure your legacy becomes reality?

2

Hang on Little Cowboy

*Desire that your life count for something great! Long for your
life to have eternal significance. Want this!
Don't coast through life without a passion." - John Piper*

In 2017 I had the privilege of speaking to elementary students in Carthage. Carthage is a great little town in southwest Missouri. KC Wolf is no stranger to this city. I have been there many times in 25 years presenting programs at several schools. On this occasion I had been invited by two of the local elementary schools to celebrate Red Ribbon Week. Red Ribbon Week is a week-long alcohol, drug and violence prevention awareness campaign which schools annually celebrate during the last week in October. Every year, Red Ribbon Week is by far the most requested week for KC Wolf school programs. It is not uncommon for me to speak at 10 or more schools during this week. Since every school requests the KC Wolf "Say No to Drug" program during this particular week, I listen to myself repeating the same information over and over again.

Carthage is a two-hour drive straight south of Kansas City, so thankfully my first program at Fairview Elementary was scheduled to start at 10:00 a.m. Let me confess, I'm not a morning person. It is always difficult for me to try to stand up in front of 350 excited kids before I am even awake. Occasionally I come across a principal who was raised on a farm and thinks every school day should begin as soon as the rooster crows; and in some small rural towns, they prefer to have their school programs first thing in the morning shortly after the students arrive. I hate to admit it, but on more than one occasion I've left my house at 5:00 a.m. drinking a Mountain Dew, eating a Pop Tart and just trying to wake up. I know it's not exactly the breakfast of champions, but some mornings I just need something to shock my system.

I finished speaking to the students at Fairview Elementary around 11:00 a.m., and my next program wasn't scheduled to begin until 1:30 p.m. at Mark Twain Elementary. With time to kill I decided to pay a surprise visit to a friend of mine who is the pastor at First Church of the Nazarene in Carthage. I had first met Dustin Ledford when I spoke at his previous church, Highway Church of the Nazarene, in the little town of Ava. I spoke there on a Sunday morning in 2004 and brought my two oldest children along with me. My oldest daughter Mycah was eight at the time, and my son Aaron was six. They were both eager to join me on the trip, not because they enjoyed listening to their dad speak but because after the church service Pastor Dustin had offered to take them horseback riding.

My children were born and raised in Kansas City which is not exactly the Wild Wild West, and Aaron was especially excited about getting to ride on a real live horse. He seemed to think since he owned a cowboy hat made out of straw and had watched an episode of the Lone Ranger early on in his young life, it somehow qualified him to be a real cowboy. On the way to church that morning all my kids talked about was riding horses. They asked me not to preach too long because they wanted to get on the horses as soon as possible.

When we arrived, the church members and staff were very welcoming. They had been planning this morning with KC Wolf for a long time. My kids got excited when they found out the church served donuts, and they weren't just ordinary glazed donuts. This church went all out! They served donuts with sprinkles on top. My kids loved the sprinkled donuts, but

I'm sure the church custodian hated them because most of the sprinkles landed on the floor. My kids also learned they could attend a Sunday School class with other kids their age instead of sitting through "big church" and listening to me preach.

After finishing their donuts one of the Sunday School teachers took them back to the children's area while I slipped into the pastor's office to put on my costume. KC Wolf paid a surprise visit to each of the children's classrooms before church started, and then I made my way into the sanctuary. I always enjoy watching people's faces when I walk into a church service dressed as KC Wolf. Occasionally a church will ask me to speak in a suit and tie, but more often than not they want me to come in dressed as KC Wolf. After my grand entrance Dustin introduced me, and I removed the costume and gave the sermon dressed in shorts and a sweaty t-shirt. Once the costume was off, I definitely wasn't the best dressed person in church.

After the service, we went directly to the horse stables. Even though it was a little bit chilly it was still a nice day to ride. Dustin lifted Aaron up on a horse and slowly led him out across the pasture. I could tell by the smile on Aaron's face that he was living the dream. I'm sure he was sitting on the trusty steed, thinking about a way to purchase a horse of his own and keep it in our third car garage at home. After several minutes it became obvious my son was very confident in his riding ability. Dustin stopped to take a short break, and what happened next has been a story we have laughed about for years.

Somehow Aaron managed to kick the horse in the ribs, and the horse took off across the pasture with Dustin and me in hot pursuit. I discovered quickly that horses are much faster than humans. There was no way I was going to catch up to my son. It was the first time in my life I had ever prayed while sprinting as fast as I could. My wide-eyed little cowboy stayed in the saddle until about halfway across the pasture, before deciding he'd had enough. He jumped off the galloping horse, landing in a heap on the cold, hard ground. Thankfully, other than a few minor bumps and bruises Aaron escaped unharmed.

From that day forward, every time I see Pastor Dustin, the first thing he always asks is, "How is your son doing?" God was definitely looking out for my son that day and answering the prayers of two grown men sprinting full speed across a pasture.

I had fun surprising Pastor Dustin at his church and catching up with him about what he and his family were doing. He even took me out to lunch at the local Mexican restaurant. I offered to pay, but he told me it was his treat. Personally, I think he was still feeling guilty about the day his horse nearly sent my son to meet Jesus.

After lunch I headed for Mark Twain Elementary, where I met a woman who had literally influenced thousands of lives. Mark Twain Elementary, sits on Main Street in Carthage, where it has been a center of education for more than a century. In 2017 the school celebrated its 100th anniversary. As if that wasn't impressive enough, the principal of the school, Mrs. Laurel Rosenthal, has worked at the school for 52 years. She taught kindergarten for 21 years, and in 2018 she began her 31st year as the school principal.

I was amazed by the love Mrs. Rosenthal had for her students and the obvious love the students and staff of Mark Twain Elementary had for her. As we visited following the program, several of the kindergarten students came up to give her a hug. I couldn't help but think about the incredible impact she must have had on countless young lives in the town of Carthage. What I admired most about Mrs. Rosenthal was the passion she still had for educating students and guiding them along the path to success.

I was curious to know just how old Mrs. Rosenthal was, but I didn't dare ask because my mother taught me that it is never polite to ask a woman her age or her weight. As I was leaving Mark Twain that day, I thanked Mrs. Rosenthal for inviting me to speak to her students. I also thanked her for making a positive impact in her little corner of the world. For 52 years at the 1400 block of South Main Street, Mrs. Laurel Rosenthal had used her time and talents to make a difference in the lives of young people.

In 2005 Steve Jobs, the co-founder of Apple Computer, gave a commencement speech at Stanford University. In his speech he said, "You've got to find what you love. The only way to do great work is to love what you do. If you haven't found it yet, keep looking. Don't settle. As with all matters of the heart, you'll know when you find it." Steve Jobs understood the importance of passion. Passion is the secret to overcoming the setbacks and struggles each of us face in life. Passion is what keeps you going even on those difficult days when you just want to throw in the towel.

I'm thankful and blessed to know people like Pastor Dustin Ledford and Principal Laurel Rosenthal. They are both passionate about serving those in their sphere of influence. As a result, the little town of Carthage is a better place to live. They taught me that if you want to live a life of influence you need to discover your passion and use it to be a blessing to others. People with passion can change the world for the better.

Becoming Mission Minded: Have you discovered your passion? How can you use your passion to make your community a better place?

3

Wiffleball
With the Old Folks

"I am going to keep having fun every day I have left because there is no other way of life. You just have to decide whether you are going to live like Tigger or Eeyore." - Randy Pausch

I have always enjoyed history, and over the years I've become really good at remembering random and useless trivia. For instance, I learned 1967 was not only the year Dan Meers was born, but it was also the year of the world's first heart transplant. The first Super Bowl was in 1967. Also, Elvis Presley married Priscilla Beaulieu in Las Vegas. I am full of useless information. My wife would tell you that isn't the only thing I am full of.

Another little known fact is that National Nursing Home Week was established by the American Health Care Association in 1967. National Nursing Home Week is a week set aside each year to celebrate the role of skilled nursing care centers caring for America's seniors and individuals with disabilities. In the United States, National Nursing Home Week is always celebrated the week after Mother's Day so it's always a very busy week for KC Wolf.

Anyone who has ever had the opportunity to spend time with the elderly knows they can be a lot of fun. Some of the funniest stories and jokes I've ever heard, along with some of the best advice, has come from time spent with senior adults.

At one of my many KC Wolf nursing home appearances I was introduced to an elderly gentleman with a great sense of humor who was as bald as a bowling ball. He smiled at me and said, "In today's world, unfortunately most people don't realize just how valuable senior adults are. Old folks are worth a fortune. They have silver in their hair, gold in their teeth, stones in their kidneys, lead in their feet and gas in their stomachs." I laughed and told him he didn't have any silver in his hair because he was slick bald. Without missing a beat, he looked at me and said, "I use to have a lot of hair and I shampooed every day with Head & Shoulders. Now I just use Mop & Glo."

I was only able to stay and visit with this gentleman for a short time, but even in the brief minutes we had together it became clear I had made friends with a man who wasn't content sitting around feeling sorry for himself. Everyone at the nursing home seemed to know "Mr. Clean," and they loved him. Even in his advanced years, he was sharing smiles and laughs with everyone he met.

Over the years I've also learned the Kansas City Chiefs truly have the greatest fans in the National Football League. I might be just a little bit biased, but I love Chiefs fans. They are crazy, fun and extremely passionate about their football team. I've discovered Chiefs fans come in all shapes, sizes and ages. Some of the Chiefs biggest and most loyal fans don't come out to Arrowhead Stadium on game day because they are sitting in wheelchairs, huddled around big screen televisions at nursing homes all over the Midwest. The nursing homes may not get quite as loud, but trust me they like to wear their red and cheer on the Chiefs just like the football faithful at Arrowhead.

Chiefs fans are famous for their tailgating on Sunday at the stadium. What you may not know is there are also a lot of great Red Friday tailgates taking place during football season at nursing homes all over the city. I know because I've been to a lot of them. Old folks like to tailgate just like the rest of the fans. Occasionally I've even seen them break out the adult beverages. The biggest difference between Arrowhead and the nursing home is if you want an adult beverage at the nursing home they don't ask to see your ID.

One of my favorite appearances every year has been the annual wiffleball game held at the Missouri Veterans Home in Cameron, MO. If Cameron sounds familiar to you that's because it's the same town I mentioned back in Chapter 1 where the special colonoscopy juice decided to kick my colon into high gear. The Missouri Veterans Home has an incredible staff serving the senior adult military veterans living in the facility. From the first time I visited the Missouri Veterans Home I could tell the staff care deeply for the residents. Each year Darcy Henry, the activity director at the home, organizes a wiffleball game sponsored by the local bank. The game is played outside in the courtyard. The staff grills hotdogs, makes popcorn and they provide plenty of soda and beer for the veterans.

The game begins with the singing of the National Anthem. Standing there dressed as KC Wolf with my hand over my heart, I thanked God for the men and women at the Veterans Home who had served our country, and I prayed for those who were currently serving in the military. I'm extremely grateful for those who serve and the sacrifices of their families so we can continue to live free in the greatest country in the world.

The game always lasts exactly one hour. After 60 minutes of eating hotdogs, drinking beer and playing wiffleball, most of the veterans are ready for a nap. As I mentioned earlier, it doesn't matter if it's before a football or a wiffleball game, senior adults enjoy tailgating just like the rest of us. During the game the staff plays defense while each veteran takes his turn hitting the ball. They hit the ball off of a tee, but since most of them are confined to their wheelchairs, they need someone to run the bases for them. Every year the staff solves this problem by bringing their children to run the bases. KC Wolf tees up the ball, the veterans hit it, and then the kids run the bases. What makes the wiffleball game special is watching the smiles on the faces of the veterans and getting to participate in a game where a five-year-old and an 85-year-old are both playing on the same team.

One of my all-time favorite KC Wolf photos was taken at Villa St. Francis nursing home in Olathe, KS. I have become good friends with Verna Jones, who is the activity director. Verna has invited me out on several occasions. I always look forward to visiting the residents at Villa St. Francis, but I especially enjoy seeing my dear friend Sister Mary Kenneth. Sister Mary is a nun who works at the nursing home. All she will tell me is she is more than 80 years old. I'm curious to know her exact age, but once again I remember my mother's advice. Never ask a woman her age or her weight. I figure this is especially true if the person in question is a Catholic nun.

What makes Sister Mary so much fun is her love for the Denver Broncos. Despite the fact that she's a nun she can talk trash with the best of them. Whenever we see each other she gives me a hard time about my Chiefs, and in return I talk smack about her Broncos. She says she prays for me to have a conversion, and I tell her I'm praying the same for her. Sister Mary is so special. She is truly one of the most joyful people I know. She loves to laugh, so on one of my visits I shared with her a nun joke my friend from church had emailed me.

A young nun who worked for a local home health care agency was out making her rounds when she ran out of gas. As luck would have it, there was a gas station just a block away.

She walked to the station to borrow a can with enough gas to start the car and drive to the station for a fill up. The attendant regretfully told her the only gas can he owned had just been loaned out, but if she would wait he was sure it would be back shortly. Since the nun was on her way to see a patient she decided not to wait and walked back to her car. After looking through her car for something to carry to the station to fill with gas she spotted a bedpan she was taking to the patient. Always resourceful, she carried it to the station, filled it with gasoline, and took it back to her car. As she was pouring the gas into the tank of her car, two men watched her from across the street. One of them turned to the other and said: "I know Jesus turned water into wine, but if that car starts I'm going to church every Sunday for the rest of my life." Just listening to Sister Mary laugh is enough to bring smiles to everyone in the room. She is a woman who just bubbles over with joy. People like Sister Mary are contagious. They make an impact on the people around them.

Sister Mary isn't the only one filled with joy at Villa St. Francis. My friends Carmen and Wilma were both 102 years old when I visited them in May 2018. They asked if they could get their picture taken with KC Wolf. I told them my wife might get jealous if she found out I was getting my picture taken with such beautiful older women. They smiled and promised me they wouldn't tell her. Before we took the picture, Carmen had a special request. She asked if she could wear my size 23 KC Wolf tennis shoes. I wasn't about to tell a 102-year-old Chiefs fan that she couldn't wear my shoes so I took them off, and the nursing staff helped place them on her feet. Every time I look at this picture it reminds me of Carmen, Wilma and Sister Mary, three very special ladies whose joyful lives help spread happiness everywhere they go.

A friend of mine sent me a story which reminded me a lot of my friends at Villa St Francis. The story was about a 92-year-old, petite, well poised and proud woman. Every morning she would wake early so she could be fully dressed by 8:00 a.m., with her hair fashionably fixed and her makeup perfectly applied, even though she is legally blind. On this day she was moving to a nursing home because her husband of 70 years had recently passed away, making the move necessary.

After several hours of waiting patiently in the lobby of the nursing home, she smiled sweetly when told her room was ready. As she maneuvered her walker to the elevator, the nurse provided a visual description of the tiny room, including the eyelet sheets which hung at her window. "I love it," she said with the enthusiasm of an eight-year-old having just been presented with a new puppy. "Mrs. Jones, you haven't seen the room; just wait," the nurse stated.

"That doesn't have anything to do with it," she replied. "Happiness is something you decide on ahead of time. Whether I like my room or not doesn't depend on how the furniture is arranged, it's how I arrange my mind. I have already decided to love it. It's a decision I make every morning when I wake up."

Like Mrs. Jones, I have a choice; I can spend the day in bed recounting the difficulty I have with the parts of my body which no longer work or get out of bed and be thankful for the ones that do. Each day is a gift. As long as my eyes open I'll focus on the new day and all the happy memories I've stored away just for this time in my life. My friend who told me this story happened to be a financial planner. He said, "Old age is like a bank account. You withdraw from what you've put into the account." His advice was to deposit a lot of happiness in your account of memories.

I'm thankful for the senior adults I've met at nursing homes all over the Midwest. I'm also thankful for friends like Sister Mary, Carmen and Wilma who help me deposit happy memories into my account. Even in their later years of life they continue to impact others by living joyfully. They are a blessing to the other residents at Villa St. Francis because of how they choose to live their lives.

Randy Pausch was an American professor at Carnegie Mellon University when he learned he had pancreatic cancer. In August 2007 he was given a terminal diagnosis and told he only had about 3-6 months of good health left. Randy became famous for an upbeat lecture he gave on September 18, 2007 titled, "The Last Lecture: Really Achieving Your Childhood Dreams."

In "The Last Lecture," Pausch mentions two of the characters in A. A. Milne's classic children's book *Winnie the Pooh*, Tigger and Eeyore. If you are familiar with the book you know Tigger bounces his way through life on his tail. He likes to say, "Bouncing is what Tiggers do best!" He is proud of his bounce in life and wants others to enjoy bouncing their way through their lives. Tigger is much more than just a bouncing and excited animal. He is joyful, optimistic and hopeful. His enthusiasm is contagious, and he wants to leave a legacy in his world. Eeyore, on the other hand, could best be described as a gloomy, negative and depressed donkey.

During his lecture, Pausch encourages his audience to think about who they are in life. He says we can either choose to live like Tigger or Eeyore. Pausch reminded everyone, even as he was dying, "We cannot change the cards we are dealt, just how we play the hand." Let me encourage you that if you want your life to have an influence on others, then play your hand like Tigger. Choose Joy!

Becoming Mission Minded: Would your family and friends say you're more like Tigger or more like Eeyore? Do you need to make any changes?

4

1,544.31
Miles of Toilet Paper

"If I wanted to make a difference…wishing for things to change wouldn't make them change. Hoping for improvements wouldn't bring them. Dreaming wouldn't provide all the answers I needed. Vision wouldn't be enough to bring transformation to me or others. Only by managing my thinking and shifting my thoughts from desire to deeds would I be able to bring about positive change. I need to go from wanting to doing."
- John Maxwell

When people ask me what I'm most proud of during my long career as KC Wolf I always respond by telling them about the number of young people I've spoken to over 30 years. Since beginning my career with the Kansas City Chiefs on June 4, 1990, I have spoken at more than 3,000 school programs all over the Midwest. This number is not an exaggeration. What is really crazy is this number doesn't include the programs I've given at libraries, churches, camps or adult groups. Sometimes I feel like the black sheep of the mascot family because mascots are not supposed to talk. I don't talk while I'm dressed as KC Wolf, but when the costume comes off I make up for lost time. When I visit schools, I start off in costume entertaining the students as they gather for the assembly. Once the students are seated I take off the costume and talk about a variety of topics including: character education, fitness & nutrition, bullying prevention, reading and Say No To Drugs, just to name a few.

I can tell I've been at this for a long time because every year I meet more and more men and women who have elementary children of their own who come up to me and say, "I still remember when you came and spoke at my elementary school." It makes me feel good knowing they still remember my visit to their school, but it also makes me feel old.

If I had to use just one word to sum up what I talk with students about, it would be choices. I always try to explain to students that the choices we make each day, big choices and even those seemingly small choices, are extremely important. Our choices determine our future.

My children went to Hazel Grove Elementary School in Lee's Summit. In the school office there was a poster hanging on the wall behind the front desk. This poster always reminded me that even the small and seemingly insignificant choices I make each day, are really very important. The poster said:

Guard your thoughts because they become your words;
Guard your words because they become your actions;
Guard your actions because they become your habits;
Guard your habits because they become your character;
Guard your character because it becomes your destiny.

The choices we make each day determine our character and our destiny. Your destiny is not determined by chance. Your destiny is determined by choice. The choices you make each day write your life's story. When you stop and think about it, each of us is authoring a life story. Every day adds another sentence in our story. Since you are the author of your story, you get to decide each day whether your sentence will end in a period, a question mark or an exclamation point. Personally, I hope to live each day so it ends with an exclamation point.

In his book *Divine Direction,* author Craig Groeschel said, "What is always true is that the decisions we make today determine the stories we tell about our lives tomorrow. Every day, all day, we make one small choice after another. And those choices just keep accumulating, each one woven into the rest, forming the tapestry that is our life story." He goes on to say, "It's the small choices no one sees that result in the big impact everyone wants."

I couldn't agree more. It's easy to think successful people got to where they are by making a few big, really important decisions. In reality it's the small choices we make each day which determine the influence and impact our lives have on others. If you want a life story you can be proud to share, I encourage you to daily make small choices which will get you one step closer to becoming the person you want to be. During my mascot career I've discovered the people who have the greatest impact on others are those who are very intentional about how they spend their time, energy and resources.

A great example of this is my friend Joe Colaizzi, the executive director of the Kansas City Rescue Mission (KCRM), which was recently renamed Shelter KC. I first met Joe when KC Wolf was asked to make an appearance and speak at a chapel service at KCRM. Joe is a difference maker who has invested more than 30 years of his life working with the homeless community in Kansas City. What impresses me most about Joe is his intentionality in continuously looking for ways to improve the lives of those who are struggling.

KCRM is a Christ-centered community offering freedom and hope to the poor and homeless in the Kansas City area. Every year more than 1,500 men come through the doors of the mission looking for assistance. These men not only receive food and shelter, but they can also enroll in KCRM's recovery program. The program lasts six months and offers Bible-based life skills classes, GED preparation, adult high school, and addiction recovery through one-on-one counseling, support groups and Bible study.

After my first visit to KCRM in 2014 I have been invited back to speak to the men in the recovery program on many occasions. Each time I visit my friends at KCRM I walk away amazed at the impact Joe Colaizzi and his staff are making in the lives of those in our city who are less fortunate. Thanks to the efforts of people like Joe, the homeless men at the Rescue Mission are discovering there can be freedom from their past and hope for their futures.

In 2013, KCRM also opened a Women's Shelter ministering to single, homeless women who struggle with addictions and mental illness. I love linking arms with people and organizations like KCRM because I know they are committed to making a positive impact in the lives of those who are hurting.

KC Wolf has partnered with and worked alongside Joe Colaizzi and his staff on many projects. In December 2015 we raised money to buy insulated long underwear to give away as Christmas gifts to the homeless. In October 2016 I had the privilege of speaking at the KCRM annual fundraising banquet. A few weeks later we held another Christmas party for the men and women who were staying at KCRM and distributed Chiefs stocking caps as gifts. When it comes to Kansas City Chiefs gear I have connections. One of the many reasons I love working for the Chiefs is they have always been very supportive of my efforts. I'm proud to work for an organization who is committed to making a difference in their community. Every year I am amazed at the generosity of our owners, the Hunt family. Chiefs founder Lamar Hunt was a very generous man. When it comes to his children and their generosity, it's obvious the apple didn't fall far from the tree.

The most memorable and fun event KC Wolf assisted with at KCRM was their annual Toilet Paper Tower Competition. In a single year, KCRM's Men's and Women's Center uses around 10,000 rolls of toilet paper, costing around $6,000. The TP Tower Competition is held each year to "wipe" this need and expense off the budget. Teams compete to collect the most toilet paper. The winner is awarded the fabulous toilet paper trophy. Yes, it is a real thing. Other awards include the highest toilet paper tower and the most elaborate toilet paper sculpture.

In 2018 I decided collecting toilet paper would be a great project for KC Wolf to get 'behind.' Yes, that pun was intended. FYI...I'm writing this chapter in a hotel room in Cincinnati and I just made myself laugh.

Anyway, back to my story. I planned to purchase $1,500 worth of toilet paper with a portion of the money I made from the sale of my book *Wolves Can't Fly*. After writing my first book I made a commitment to give all the money from the sale of my books to charities and non-profits. I do this because if anyone ever buys one of my books and thinks I'm a terrible author, at least they can feel good knowing their money is going to a good cause. I was curious to find out how many rolls of toilet paper I could buy for $1,500. I had never bought this much toilet paper at one time and it sounded like a fun way to support a great cause. Besides, I couldn't wait to watch the cashier's face when I came strolling through the checkout line with $1,500 worth of toilet paper.

As I started researching where I could get the best deal on toilet paper I happened to mention the Toilet Paper Challenge to a friend of mine at church. He suggested teaming up with a local school in our community to see if we could collect even more toilet paper. I called my friend Laura Maxwell, who works for the Lee's Summit School District, and she connected me with Jennifer Kevern and Kristi Fate. Jennifer is the principal at Trailridge Elementary School and Kristi is the assistant director of the Before & After School program, in the Lee's Summit School District. Jennifer and Kristi were excited about using the Toilet Paper Challenge as a fun way to teach students about the importance of doing kind things for others.

Trailridge Elementary has more than 470 students, and Jennifer worked with her PTA to help organize the collection of toilet paper donated by the students and their families. Jennifer also reached out to Cindy Wilson, one of the managers at the local Cosentino's Price Chopper grocery store. Price Chopper then contacted Scotts Toilet Tissue company, who loved the idea and agreed to match all the toilet paper we collected. At the same time, Kristi organized the Before & After School program coordinators at the other 17 elementary schools in the Lee's Summit School District and started collecting toilet paper.

For three weeks I watched a snowball of kindness gain momentum. By the time all was said and done this amazing team collected more than 16,500 rolls of toilet paper. I must confess it was a lot more toilet paper than I originally anticipated. I started to do a little research and learned a single roll of Scotts 1000 sheet toilet paper is 302 feet long, and if you spread out a roll of the Scotts 1000 sheet toilet paper it would cover approximately 115.2 square feet. I multiplied 16,500 rolls of toilet paper by 302 feet and discovered we had collected more than 4,983,000 feet of toilet paper. I then divided the number by 5,280 feet, which is the number of feet in a mile and learned we had collected 943.75 miles of toilet paper. I asked Siri, my cell phone friend who knows everything, and she told me this was enough toilet paper to stretch from Kansas City to Washington DC as the crow flies. I was extremely proud of the students because I knew this many miles of toilet paper would wipe butts for a long time at the rescue mission. Thankfully it all came packaged in rolls, because I had 1,900,800 square feet of toilet paper to deliver.

Then it dawned on me that I needed to figure out a way to transport all of the toilet paper down to KCRM. I started making a list of every guy I knew who owned a pickup truck. I was relieved when my friends at Price Chopper offered to deliver the toilet paper to KCRM using one of their box trucks. Several other churches and youth groups from around Kansas City also participated in the KCRM Toilet Paper Challenge. When all the toilet paper was counted, the final tally was more than 27,000 rolls, which equated to a grand total of 1,544.31 miles.

Synergy is defined as 'the creation of a whole that is greater than the simple sum of its parts.' Human synergy relates to teamwork. I once heard it described like this: Person A alone is too short to reach an apple in a tree. Person B is also too short to reach the apple. However, if Person B sits on the shoulders of Person A, they are tall enough to pick the apple. The product of their synergy is one apple.

When caring individuals and companies work together to make a positive impact in their community it's fun to watch synergy in action. I smile when I think about a mascot reaching out to an after school coordinator and an elementary school principal, who then involved a lot of awesome students and a local grocery store, who reached out and teamed up with a toilet paper company. The next thing you know the local homeless shelter has enough toilet paper to wipe rear ends for a long, long time. That's synergy in action, and it's awesome!

I'm encouraged by people like Joe Colaizzi, Laura Maxwell, Jennifer Kevern, Kristi Fate, Cindy Wilson, the Cosentino family, Scott's Tissue Company and all the great students in the Lee's Summit School District who worked together. Because of their generosity, the Kansas City Rescue Mission doesn't have to worry about budgeting for toilet paper anytime soon. Instead of spending budget money on something that gets flushed down a toilet, KCRM can now use donations to continue touching lives and providing hope to those who are homeless in our community.

Becoming Mission Minded: Where in your community have you seen a need you could help meet? Who could you team up with to meet this need?

5

Freezin' My Fanny

"I feel the capacity to care is the thing which gives
life its deepest significance." - Pablo Casals

If you ask any mascot the worst part of the job, they will likely tell you it's the heat. Mascots hate hot weather. I have suffered through many long, miserably hot football games during my Chiefs career. There have been several occasions when the Chiefs training staff gives me an IV because my body is showing obvious signs of dehydration following a game. I never enjoy getting a needle stuck in my arm, but it is much less painful than the muscle cramps that accompany dehydration.

One of those miserably hot games happened very early in my career. On September 9, 1990, the Chiefs played their opening day game against the Minnesota Vikings. The temperatures were well into the upper 90's all afternoon. What made things even worse was the Chiefs played their games in those days on Astroturf. The trouble with turf was it radiated heat and made the temperature on the field significantly hotter. Even if there was a breeze blowing on the field it felt as if someone was blowing a blazing hair dryer in your face. I remember walking off the field at the end of the game having second thoughts about my chosen career path. Thankfully I survived, and the Chiefs enjoyed cooler temperatures for the remaining games that season.

The absolute worst game I ever suffered through happened 10 years later. In September 2000 my family bought a new house. The week after we moved in I spent a Saturday afternoon cleaning brush and weeds out of the backyard. Of course, I removed my shirt to show off my muscles in case my wife was watching out the kitchen window. I'm just kidding; I'm not exactly eye candy with my shirt off. I actually took my shirt off because, once again, it was a very hot September day. The first mistake I made was forgetting to put on my sunscreen. The second mistake was failing to recognize the weeds I was cleaning out of my backyard contained poison ivy. The following day I paid a high price for my stupidity.

The Chiefs had a home game, and the weather was still extremely hot, but the worst part was that under my costume I was severely sunburned and itching like crazy with poison ivy. No amount of Aloe Vera or anti itch cream seemed to help. I felt like rubbing against the goal post like a bear using a tree to scratch his back, but I didn't think this would look appropriate in front of the Chiefs fans. I don't remember whether the Chiefs won or lost the game, but I do remember it was the longest and most miserable three hours of my entire career. It was a heavy price paid for going shirtless and trying to impress my wife.

Occasionally people ask if I get cold while dressed as KC Wolf. The only time I ever remember being extremely frigid in costume was when the Cass County Sheriff's Department invited me to participate in the annual Polar Bear Plunge.

The Polar Bear Plunge is a fundraiser whose proceeds benefit Missouri Special Olympics' year-round program of sports training and competition for children and adults with intellectual disabilities. The officers at the Sheriff's Department are a great group of guys who care deeply for their community. They are always actively involved in helping with local causes, and over the years I have enjoyed working with them. The sheriff knew KC Wolf is a sucker when it comes to having fun and promoting good causes, so doing the Polar Bear Plunge seemed like a great idea. That is, until I realized the plunge would occur in January. January in Missouri is typically cold, and this year it happened to be frigid.

When I went to the Polar Bear Plunge website to get signed up it said: "This 'unbearable' event is a unique opportunity to show your bravery as you support local Special Olympics athletes by walking, running or crawling into the frigid winter waters." Some call it bravery and others call it stupidity, but all I remember is I had a lot of fun. When I arrived at the beach at Longview Lake there was a big sign that read 'Freezin' for a Reason' It was obvious everyone was going to have a good time, and the festive atmosphere surrounding the event made me (briefly) forget how cold it was.

I slipped into the men's locker room to put on my KC Wolf costume, and since I really wanted to impress people, I dressed KC Wolf up in a red speedo swimsuit and a gaudy green Hawaiian shirt. I knew anyone with 85 inch hips and as much body hair as I had would definitely turn some heads if I came walking out in a tight red speedo.

Sure enough, when I stepped out of the locker room I immediately got a reaction. As the crowd gathered around me I spent the first 15 minutes getting pictures taken with other participants, and I stayed warm until it was my turn to make the plunge. Then it was my turn. Jogging casually into the water, I was fine until the water started to seep into my costume. When the frigid, ice cold water hit my crotch I began to question whether this had been a good idea. My legs were already going numb, and I recalled a horrifying story in the newspaper about a man who got frostbite while climbing a mountain and the doctors had to amputate his big toe. I was starting to think KC Wolf might be the next amputee. Fueled by the energy of those around me, I continued my plunge into the lake, the cold water literally took my breath away. I could sense several body parts were starting to turn blue. I stayed in the lake just long enough to get a picture taken and quickly headed back to shore. Once on shore I posed for a few more quick pictures with my family and headed toward the men's locker room to take off my heavy, wet fur. After getting dressed and bundled up in my winter coat, gloves and hat, I headed back to the beach to watch others making the plunge.

While I warmed up, I listened to the music and looked around at the hundreds of volunteers and other people dressed in crazy outfits. I was encouraged to see so many people who cared enough to get involved. It would have been much easier for these folks to stay at home in their nice warm houses, drinking hot chocolate in front of a fire. Instead, they took the time out of their weekend to get involved with a good cause and make a positive difference in the lives of others. I talked with one man who had been taking the plunge for several years. I asked him what kept him coming back. He replied, "It's always fun and I've been able to make some great memories with my family over the years. Plus, it's just a small way I can help out a great cause." His comment reminds me when you get enough people together who are willing to give just a little, it can make a big difference. I'm grateful for my friends at the Sheriff's Department who invited me to get involved, because it was an experience I won't soon forget.

In 2016 I had the honor of working with another group of very caring police officers in Lee's Summit. Lee's Summit is a suburb of Kansas City, and it holds a special place in my heart because my wife and I have lived there since 1994. Each year the Lee's Summit Police Department raises money and donations for their Shop with a Cop program. Thanks to sales from my previous book we were able to help with a financial donation. Shop with a Cop is a program assisting economically less fortunate youth during the holiday season. The police department works with the local school district to identify underprivileged students. The basics of the program include a police officer picking up a child and accompanying them to the local Walmart where each child receives money to purchase Christmas gifts for themselves and their family. Once the gifts are purchased, the officer brings the child back to the police station where they eat pizza and cookies and spend time wrapping the gifts. As I watched the Lee's Summit police officers interacting with the children, it was obvious this is much more than just a job for them. These officers are doing what they can to help make Christmas a special time for the kids.

I have met many police officers during my mascot career, not only at special events like Shop with a Cop and Polar Bear Plunge, but also on highways and interstates all over the Midwest. I spend a lot of time on the road traveling to my appearances. At times I have been known to travel a bit too quickly. On several occasions I have been stopped by policemen and handed a slip of paper informing me to slow down. I can honestly say that each time I'm handed a slip of paper I deserve it, even though I'm not always excited to send in the mandatory donation.

I have a tremendous amount of respect for the men and women who wear a badge and protect our communities. It's a difficult job, and I'm grateful they hold people like me accountable when I make a bad choice. If I choose to drive too fast, I deserve a ticket. It's not the officer's fault I got a ticket; it's my fault. Growing up, my parents taught me that my choices in life always come with consequences. They were right. As a kid if I made a bad choice there was a punishment. My butt hurt. Now that I'm an adult, when I make a bad choice, my wallet hurts. I've tried to pass this same lesson on to my own kids.

While I have a great deal of respect for police officers, I'm also guilty of giving them a hard time at Chiefs games. One of my favorite KC Wolf outfits is my police uniform. Occasionally I will dress KC Wolf in his cop outfit and walk out on the sidelines carrying a box of donuts. When police officers working security on the sidelines see me coming, they know I'm about to give them the business. I set the box of donuts down in front of them and slowly step away. As I step away, I look at the officers and then look back down at the donuts, as if to say, "Go ahead and have a donut." What the officers don't know is I have a piece of fishing line tied to the donut box. When they reach for a donut, I pull the box away. The crowd always enjoys a good laugh watching KC Wolf messing with the police officers, who are always very good sports.

As with any occupation or group of people, if you look hard enough, you're going to find a bad apple. However, I've discovered the vast majority of police officers are very caring individuals who work hard to help protect and serve their communities. KC Wolf may cheer for the boys wearing red Chiefs jerseys, but I'm also a big fan of the boys in blue.

Becoming Mission Minded: What is something you can do to say thank you to those who serve in your community? Don't just sit there. Go do it.

6

Hit by a Stoplight

"I'm so optimistic I'd go after Moby Dick in a row boat and take the tartar sauce with me." - Zig Ziglar

In 1990 I became a member of a very intriguing club, comprised of a small group of professionals scattered around the United States who wear suits to work. What makes this group unique is instead of wearing ties with our suits, most of us wear tails. What I love most about this club is almost every member is extremely optimistic. We love to laugh and have fun. Our view on life is the cup is always half full. The name of the club is "The Furternity," and it's made up of mascots of all sizes, shapes and colors.

To become an official member of The Furternity you have to work either full time or part time for a sports franchise. Some Furternity members work in the minor leagues, while others like me work for professional teams. Since there are many different sports, The Furternity is subdivided into specialty groups. There is the NBA Furternity for mascots who perform at professional basketball games, the MLB Furternity for professional baseball mascots and the NHL Furternity for hockey mascots. However, my favorite, and the one I am a member of, is the NFL Furternity. Although I am good friends with Furternity members in the other leagues, the guys I spend the most time with are my NFL Furternity brothers.

Many professional fields such as health care, counseling and finance require their employees to take continuing education classes each year. Although being a certified member of the NFL Furternity doesn't require any continuing education credits, we do like to get together occasionally to talk business (monkey business) and have fun. Every year we have our annual NFL Mascot conference where we discuss critically important mascot topics such as: skits, giveaways, sponsorship promotions, social media ideas and the latest spray deodorant strong enough to kill the smell of a sweaty costume.

The breakout session I always look forward to most is on mascot props. Members of The Furternity are extremely creative, and we are always coming up with new prop ideas. My favorite was the year I learned about the Toilet Paper Gun. It consists of a battery-operated leaf blower with a paint roller duct taped to the end of it. You load the gun by placing a roll of toilet paper onto the paint roller directly in front of the blower. When you pull the trigger on the leaf blower, the toilet paper will shoot out in one continuous stream. It works great at sporting events! I wish I would have discovered the toilet paper gun 30 years earlier, because back in high school it would have made TPing my friends' houses so much easier.

In 2016, the NFL mascot conference was held in Indianapolis. Trey Mock (aka Blue) is the mascot for the Indianapolis Colts, and he offered to host the conference. Not only is Trey a nice guy and a talented mascot, we quickly learned he was also a great event planner. He took our annual conference to a whole new level.

One of the elements Trey added to the conference was an annual NFL Mascots vs. Peewees football game. The proceeds from the game support Make-A-Wish of Ohio, Kentucky and Indiana. It's exciting to see so many fans show up to watch a bunch of grown men dressed in feathers and fur competing against Peewee football players. The mascots are unquestionably bigger, but the kids are faster and can definitely see better. More often than not the Peewees win the game. The best part of the evening is when the mascots and Peewees come together after the game to present a check to the Make-A-Wish Foundation. Once again, it always reminds me of the impact a group of people can have when they get together to have fun and support a good cause.

Another element added by Trey to our annual conference was the NFL Mascot Awards. At the conference, each NFL Furternity brother votes on who they think deserves each of the NFL Mascot Awards. In 2016 there were five different categories:

- Stunt of the Year
- Skit of the Year
- Video of the Year
- Social Media Post of the Year
- Mascot of the Year

On the final night of the conference, the mascots all go for a nice dinner at Harry & Izzy's restaurant. After dinner, Trey stood up to announce the award winners. Before giving out the awards, he mentioned there was one other special new award he wanted to present. He said the award was being given to an individual highly respected by his peers who had made a huge impact on the NFL Mascot community. While my Furternity brothers sat around the room with silly grins on their faces, I sat there clueless.

Trey announced the award going to be called the NFL Mascot Dan Meers Lifetime Achievement Award. As soon as the words left his mouth everyone started cheering, and I sat in my chair with tears welling up in my eyes. I didn't know anything about the award, and I didn't get to vote on who deserved it. Trey said since the award was named after me I should probably be the first one to receive it.

What made the award even more special was Trey had compiled a video of former and current Furternity members I had worked with over my then 27-year career. They had each taken time to send in a short video clip congratulating me and roasting me on the award. After the video Trey had another surprise. He got everyone's attention and proposed a toast. When I looked up, all of my Furternity brothers were holding shot glasses filled with 2% milk. They knew I didn't drink alcohol so they ordered up 30 shot glasses filled with milk. It was a mascot conference I will never forget.

Trey did such an outstanding job hosting the 2016 NFL Mascot conference that we voted to return to Indianapolis again the following year. In 2017, I was again humbled with a first-time award. I was selected as the inaugural winner of the 'NFL Mascot Anchor in the Community Award' for my charitable efforts in Kansas City and my work with orphanages around the world. It felt good to be recognized for my efforts, but I also knew there were many other NFL mascots from around the country who deserved to receive the same award.

Our conferences aren't the only times the NFL Furternity gets together. Occasionally we are invited by the league to special events. One such event was the opening of the NFL Experience in Times Square in New York City. The NFL Experience was advertised as an interactive, museum-style attraction where football fans could experience what it is like to play in the NFL. The league hoped it would become a tourist attraction for NFL fans visiting the Big Apple, and the league invited all NFL Mascots to New York to help promote the grand opening. Seventeen of my Furternity brothers showed up, and the league put us up in the Renaissance Hotel in the heart of Times Square. Our first night together was spent sitting in a restaurant eating, drinking and trading our latest mascot stories. Around 1:00 a.m. I walked back to my hotel room to get some sleep. I noticed lights kept flashing on the ceiling in my room, and when I opened the shades, I discovered my window overlooked the M & M store; the huge neon sign beneath me had thousands of flashing lights. I discovered firsthand how difficult it is trying to fall asleep in the city that never sleeps.

The next morning the hotel lobby filled up with mascots appearing out of the elevators. The NFL decided the best way to transport 17 mascots around New York was on two double decker buses. Since mascot costumes are tall and most have big heads, everyone immediately climbed the stairs to the top floor of the double decker bus. The other reason every mascot preferred the top of the bus was because there was a slight breeze blowing in our faces as we traveled between locations.

On this trip I happened to get on the same bus with Pat the Patriot, the mascot for the New England Patriots. Now the people in Boston might have loved Pat, but in New York most people cheer for the Jets and the Giants. I quickly learned Pat the Patriot was not well liked in New York. As we drove toward the Empire State Building, our buses were attracting a lot of attention. Apparently seeing 17 mascots standing on top of two buses during rush hour traffic was an unusual sight, even in the Big Apple.

Whenever people walking on the sidewalk would recognize Pat the Patriot, they would yell insults. New Yorkers called Pat many names, some of which would cause even a veteran sailor to blush. Of course Pat was a mascot who couldn't talk, so he just continued waving to the crowd from atop the bus, sporting the big mascot grin permanently plastered on his face.

As we neared the Empire State Building, we came to an intersection where the bus had to stop because of a red light. The buses were sitting in the left turn lane waiting for the light to turn green. This particular intersection contained a large number of very vocal New Yorkers expressing their dislike of Pat and the New England Patriots. As they screamed obscenities and Pat continued to wave, the light turned green and the buses rounded the corner. Unfortunately for Pat, he was so preoccupied with the crowd that he failed to see a second stoplight hanging across the street. Several other mascots ducked out of the way to avoid the stoplight, but Pat failed to move and got smacked right in the side of the head. The New Yorkers erupted with laughter as Pat bent over, rubbing his head. I must admit I also busted out laughing as I watched the scene unfold. As the bus continued down the street, I looked back to see the stoplight swinging wildly and a bunch of happy New Yorkers laughing at Pat's misfortune. Thankfully Pat's mascot head consisted of a helmet with foam built around it. The only thing hurt that day was Pat's pride. Much to Pat's chagrin, many of the NFL Furternity brothers witnessed the whole incident, which meant the story of Pat and the New York stoplight went down in mascot folklore.

Another opportunity for the NFL Furternity to get together each year is at the Pro Bowl. The Pro Bowl is the NFL's version of an All-Star game and is normally held in late January, the week prior to the Super Bowl. Although the Pro Bowl has been played in several different locations over the years, my favorite is when it is held in Honolulu.

Even though the Pro Bowl is considered a week-long work trip, for me it never really feels like work. There is never a dull moment when you are hanging out with your Furternity brothers in Hawaii. Most of the week is spent doing appearances around the island to help promote the game. However, when we aren't in costume, you can usually find us in our swimsuits hanging out on Waikiki Beach. Since it is winter most of us haven't seen the sun in a long time, and it shows when we take our shirts off. I always like lying on the beach next to my Furternity brother from the Minnesota Vikings because he is so white he makes everybody else look tan.

One of the traditions we started at the Pro Bowl in Hawaii is the NFL Mascot calendar shoot. Each year most NFL teams have cheerleading squads that travel to tropical locations to shoot their annual cheerleader calendar. We decided if the cheerleaders could make a calendar, the mascots should as well.

Since we were already in Hawaii, we located a great spot for our calendar shoot. We drove up to the North Shore to a secluded beach area where we could take photos and shared lots of laughs as we dressed in wigs and did our best to look sexy. Our final pose was a group shot of the NFL Furternity dressed in outlandish swimwear, with ocean waves crashing onto the shore behind us. We didn't exactly look like supermodels, but we had fun pretending to be.

In November 2018 I had the privilege of participating in the annual MLB Mascot conference at Kauffman Stadium in Kansas City. My good friend Brad Collins, who works as Sluggerr, the Kansas City Royals mascot, asked if I would give the MLB Furternity members a tour of Arrowhead Stadium and then speak to them about my career. I was excited about the opportunity to be with my furry friends. Not only would I get to meet some of the newest MLB mascots, I would also have a chance to catch up with my friend Drake Fenlon. Drake worked for me as a backup KC Wolf a few years earlier and went on to become Stomper, the mascot for the Oakland Athletics.

After my presentation I stuck around for part of the conference. I was impressed when I learned of all the charity work the MLB mascots were helping with in their communities. I knew NFL mascots were involved with many different charity efforts, and I was encouraged to hear the MLB mascots were doing the same. While many people watch mascots perform at sporting events, they often are unaware of the good causes we help support throughout the week. From nursing home and hospital visits to charity events and fundraisers, one of the most rewarding parts of a mascot's job is to serve as a goodwill ambassador for their team.

Saturday, April 6, 2019 was an exciting day for current and former mascots around the world because it was the day we cut the ribbon at the Mascot Hall of Fame in Whiting, IN. The Mascot Hall of Fame was originally established in 2005. KC Wolf was honored to be selected as a member of the second class inducted into the Mascot Hall of Fame in August 2006. My good friend Dave Raymond, who was the original Phillie Phanatic, mascot of the Philadelphia Phillies, from 1978 to 1993, founded the Mascot Hall of Fame. It was originally founded as an online–only Hall of Fame, with an induction ceremony which took place in Philadelphia.

I remember the day I stood in Love Park in Philadelphia alongside my friend Clutch the Bear from the Houston Rockets and Jazz Bear from the Utah Jazz. We were each handed The Golden Silly String Award as part of our induction ceremony. It is by far the most unique trophy I've ever received.

Dave Raymond is a man I have known and respected for a long time. He has always been one of the leading spokesmen and supporters of mascots across the nation. His mascot camps have taught hundreds of aspiring mascots the tricks of the trade. Dave is full of passion and energy, so it didn't surprise me when he gathered enough support and resources to create a Mascot Hall of Fame building.

In 2014 Dave signed an agreement with the city of Whiting, IN to develop a permanent Mascot Hall of Fame building on the south shore of Lake Michigan. The mission of the Mascot Hall of Fame is to honor mascot performers, performances and programs which have positively affected their communities. The Mascot Hall of Fame also partnered with the Boys and Girls Clubs and held an online auction which contributed to the cause. Most of the items auctioned were one of a kind mascot items or pieces of signed sports memorabilia donated by sports teams from around the nation. Once again it felt good to know a group of mascots joined together to help support a good cause. It had been 13 years since I received the Golden Silly String Award, so on the day I arrived for the ribbon cutting on the permanent Mascot Hall of Fame building, I was filled with pride. I can only imagine how Dave Raymond felt.

I am proud to be a member of The Furternity. My colleagues in feathers and fur play characters for a living. Most of these men are characters in real life. What really makes them special to me is their optimistic outlook. They use their influence as professional mascots to make a positive impact in the lives of others. They spread laughter and love to people all across the country. I respect each one of them, regardless of what sport or team they cheer for.

Becoming Mission Minded: Not everyone can be a member of The Furternity, but there are many other fun clubs you can join that are making a big difference in communities all across the nation. Rotary Club, Lion's Club, Sertoma, Kiwanis Club, and Optimist Club are just a few of the many great organizations that promote service over self. Why not join a service club today? It's a great way to make new friends and have a positive impact on others in your community.

7

Skydiving With
Two of My Little Pigs

"Living with fear stops us from taking risks, and if you don't go out on the branch, you're never going to get the best fruit." - Sarah Parish

During my years as a mascot I've invested a lot of time, energy and effort into my occupation. If I could live my life over again, I would choose the exact same job, working for the exact same team. I love my career choice, and I love working for the Kansas City Chiefs.

However, anyone who knows me very well knows that being KC Wolf is not my favorite job. The best job in the world is being a father to the three greatest kids in the world. My oldest daughter Mycah was born in 1996. My son Aaron came along in 1998, and then God blessed us with Mallory in 2001. I quickly learned nothing in life can adequately prepare a man to become a father. It didn't take long for me to discover being a good dad was a lot like being a good mascot. Not only was it going to require time, energy and effort to do the job right, but it was also going to take a lot of blood, sweat, tears and prayers. Although being a dad has proven to be my most challenging job, it is also by far the most rewarding.

I have had so many priceless moments with my kids. In 2002 I joined my kids for Halloween. We walked around our neighborhood dressed as KC Wolf and the Three Little Pigs. Our evening together was priceless. Another highlight was when each of my kids was in kindergarten. They each asked if

I would bring KC Wolf to visit their classroom for show and tell. Performing at Chiefs football games can't compare to the joy I felt watching the smiles on my kids' faces when they got to show off KC Wolf to their friends at school. I have always tried to use my platform as KC Wolf to impact the lives of young people, but I also realize my greatest calling is to be a positive influence in the lives of my own children. Making an impact in the lives of others always begins with those closest to you.

As my children grew older, one of the biggest lessons I tried to teach them was to live life by faith and not by fear. In my own life I have found some of life's greatest experiences are on the opposite side of fear. For example, when I was first offered the position working as KC Wolf, I almost turned it down. I had grown up in St. Charles, MO, close to St. Louis. That was where all my family lived, and it was my comfort zone. The thought of moving 225 miles away to Kansas City was scary because I didn't really know anyone there. At times, even after accepting the Chiefs offer, I still had fears and doubts. Looking back, I'm thankful I chose to face my fear, get out of my comfort zone and accept the job with the Chiefs. It ended up being one of the greatest decisions of my life.

Another example I often have shared with my children about facing fear is when I met their mother. When I was first introduced to Cam I was afraid to ask her out because I figured she was out of my league. She was. Even though I was fearful, I worked up enough courage to finally ask her on a date. The rest is history. Being married to Cam has also turned out to be one of the greatest experiences of my life.

The longer I parent, the more I realize my kids learn best by example. As my kids aged, I knew if I was going to talk to them about overcoming fear then I should also model it for them.

Skydiving had always been on my bucket list, but the thought of jumping out of a perfectly good airplane scared me to death. As you may know, I attempted a bungee jump back in 2013 at Arrowhead Stadium, and that jump didn't turn out very well for me. (For the complete story on my bad bungee jump, see my first book entitled *Wolves Can't Fly*). So the thought of going skydiving definitely stirred deep feelings of fear in me. I finally made the decision to face my fear of skydiving during the summer of 2019, and I invited my kids to join me. Once again, it was time for my kids to see their dad practice what he preached. Mallory was only 17 at the time. In the United States you have to be 18 to jump out of a plane. Mycah, who was always my most cautious child, told me there was no way she was going to jump out of an airplane, but she would go along and watch. Aaron was my last hope. After a little convincing, he finally agreed to join me on my adventure.

The following week I called Falcon Skydiving and reserved a time for Aaron and me to jump. I then called Aaron and told him I had put down a nonrefundable deposit on our skydive. I knew Aaron was nervous about the jump because earlier in the week he sent me a text message. He said he had woken up in the middle of the night, and when he thought about jumping out of a plane he felt sick.

When I talked to Aaron I couldn't pass up the opportunity to mess with him. I told him Falcon Skydiving was a very reputable company that had been in business for 14 years, and in all those years they had only lost three people. After I said it, Aaron got really quiet on the phone. He had bit on my lie–hook, line and sinker. I could hardly keep from laughing as I continued talking as if losing three people in 14 years was no big deal.

After going on and on, I finally told him I had been pulling his leg and no one had actually died at Falcon Skydiving. I heard Aaron breathe a huge sigh of relief over the phone as he said, "Dad, you scared me to death. I was about to tell you there was no way I was going to go skydiving."

I laughed and assured Aaron skydiving was actually very safe. We were each going to be doing a tandem jump with instructors who had skydived thousands of times. I also informed him every instructor had a backup parachute just in case the first parachute malfunctioned.

After doing a little research, we learned only one in every 500,000 tandem skydives ends in death. We also discovered, according to the National Safety Council, a person is more likely to be killed by lightning or a bee sting than in a skydiving accident. Aaron decided he liked his odds well enough to go along with me. I told him we would bring along some wasp spray just to make sure we made it home alive.

On the day of the jump I woke up early and went downstairs to eat breakfast. The house was quiet, which didn't help relieve the anxiety I was feeling. Since Mycah and Aaron both lived away at college, they were making the early morning drive back home. Cam and Mallory were out of town and were going to miss out on our big jump. In the quietness of my home I sat at the kitchen table eating breakfast. I tried to take my mind off the fact that I was about to jump out of an airplane in a few hours. I sent out a group text to a few good friends asking them to pray for us. I told them I was listening to the song 'I Believe I Can Fly.' My friend Wilm Hanna made me laugh when he texted back and said a more appropriate song might be 'Another One Bites The Dust.' After breakfast I went back upstairs and put on my Superman boxer shorts. I figured if I was going to jump out of a plane and fly through the air, wearing Superman boxers would only be appropriate.

Mycah arrived home from Springfield, MO around 10:30 a.m., and Aaron and his girlfriend Kyndal showed up 30 minutes later. When I asked Aaron if he wanted anything for breakfast he told me he had already eaten a bunch of leftovers from the previous night. I laughed out loud when he told me he and Kyndal had gone out for a nice dinner the night before in case it was his last supper.

We arrived early at Falcon Skydiving so we could fill out paperwork and go through the training class. While we waited, I talked with one of the certified tandem jumpmasters. He had made over 5,000 jumps and assured us skydiving was extremely safe. He also told us it would be an experience we would never forget. It was obvious he was a man who was passionate about skydiving.

When the training class began, Aaron and I went into a small building with another one of the instructors while Mycah and Kyndal stayed outside visiting with the jumpmaster. As Aaron and I filled out our paperwork I heard a familiar voice say, "Dad." When I turned around I couldn't believe my eyes. Mycah had decided to join in on the fun.

I'm not sure what the jumpmaster said to convince Mycah to skydive, but he deserves to win salesman of the century. As a child Mycah never liked to ride anything fast because it scared her to death. Somehow this man talked my daughter into jumping out of an airplane and free falling at 124 miles per hour. If Aaron and I were nervous, I knew Mycah was really out of her comfort zone. I was beyond thrilled, knowing I was going to get to share this experience with my two oldest children. When the training was over, we put on our parachute harnesses. As we were getting fitted with our equipment several dear friends showed up. Rod Handley, along with Wilm and Tanya Hanna, made a special trip to surprise us and watch us make the jump. They know my family very well, so they were totally shocked when they learned Mycah was also going to skydive. As we stood there visiting there was plenty of nervous laughter.

Once we were ready to go, we followed the jumpmasters onto the runway and loaded into the small plane. When the door closed and the plane started to take off my heart began beating a little faster. The reality of what we were about to do began to sink in. They informed us that after takeoff we would be climbing to almost three miles in the air. After we jumped, we would free fall for two miles in the first 60 seconds, reaching speeds up to 124 miles per hour. At that point the jumpmasters would deploy the parachutes. It would then take approximately five additional minutes for us to reach the ground. When we reached an altitude of 14,000 feet, they slid open the door of the plane, and there was a sudden blast of cold air. We watched as the first two skydivers confidently made the leap. It was obvious they had jumped out of airplanes many times before. Everyone else in our group were first time tandem jumpers. We all sat wide-eyed, attached to our jumpmasters. The instructors knew Mycah was the most nervous. They didn't want to give her a lot of time to sit and think, so she was the first to go. As they exited the plane I heard a scream, and Mycah disappeared from my sight. Next up was Aaron, who also looked a little pale, but he bravely made the leap without screaming. I was next in line. I knew if both my kids had already jumped there was no way I could turn back now. We walked to the open door, and as I got into position I suddenly forgot everything I had just learned in the skydiving training session. Even though my brain had decided to shut off, my heart was working overtime.

What happened next is hard to put into words. As we jumped from the plane and started plummeting toward the ground, I felt another strong blast of cold air. I heard what sounded like a very loud freight train. When my brain finally decided to reengage, the first thought to enter my mind was maybe I should have worn a pair of Depends instead of my Superman boxers. Even though our instructor told us to take it all in and try to enjoy the moment, I discovered his words were a lot easier said than done. As we continued free falling I wasn't the least bit worried about getting killed by a bee sting because I knew there was no way a bee could fly as fast as I was traveling.

I should also mention, I had signed up to get a video and pictures of our skydiving adventure so we would have proof of our bravery/stupidity. A Go Pro camera was attached to the jumpmaster's left arm. I wanted to make sure I got some good pictures, so while I was falling, I turned my head to the left and attempted to look directly into the camera. As soon as I smiled, my lips started flapping in the wind. It felt like some-one had a hair dryer set on the highest setting, and it was blowing straight into my mouth. Within seconds my lips were completely dried out.

After free falling for what seemed like an eternity the jump-master finally deployed the parachute. I felt a sudden jerk on my harness, and then I got the biggest wedgie of my life. Even though the wedgie was uncomfortable, it was worth it know-ing the parachute was doing what it was designed to do. As we floated toward our landing area I took a few deep breaths and tried to enjoy the ride. The ride was much more relaxing and enjoyable once my lips were no longer flapping in the wind.

As we floated closer to the ground I could see my friends waving from the viewing area. My jumpmaster reminded me to lift my legs and keep my feet straight out in front of me as we landed. I did exactly as I was told, and I came sliding in on my butt for a perfect landing. As I stood to my feet I could see Mycah walking in my direction. I embraced her and gave her a huge hug. The first thing out of her mouth was, "I'm never doing that again." I told her I was very proud of her. She had faced her fear with amazing courage and had overcome it. Even though Aaron had jumped before me, he was the last to land. He came walking toward Mycah and me with a huge grin on his face. All three of us were very thankful to have our feet back on the ground. As we were preparing to leave, the instructor handed us each a certificate. Mine said, "This is to certify that Dan Meers has successfully completed a tandem skydive." It was signed by my instructor, Aaron Mitchell. Although he had done all the work getting us safely back on the ground, I also felt a huge sense of accomplishment knowing I had completed my first skydive. We took our certificates and proudly posed for a family photo. It was late afternoon and we hadn't eaten anything since breakfast, so we stopped for a celebration dinner on the way home.

As I reflected on the day's activities I was reminded of a quote by the famous South African anti–apartheid revolutionary and political leader Nelson Mandela. He once said, "I learned that courage was not the absence of fear, but the triumph over it. The brave man is not he who does not feel afraid, but he who conquers that fear." I was a proud father that day. Even though I knew my kids were afraid of skydiving, they had faced their fear and conquered it.

I know Mycah and Aaron will never forget the day their dad took them skydiving. It was definitely one of the most memorable days of my life as well. I still sit down with my kids and watch the videos so we can relive our fall from the sky. Plus, every time I wear my Superman boxers I think back to our special day. I hope my kids learned a valuable lesson that day about facing fear. My prayer is it will stick with them throughout their lives. I want my kids to grow up to be difference makers in their world, living by faith and not fear.

Many times fear keeps people in their comfort zones. It keeps them from living a life of impact and influence. Simple things like volunteering at a homeless shelter or working at a food pantry can feel awkward at first. Going overseas and serving at an orphanage where the children don't speak your language can be frightening. Getting involved and reaching out to those who are hurting can make you feel uneasy and uncomfortable. I know because I've experienced it many times, but just like my skydiving adventure I've never regretted stepping out and making the leap. I've discovered some of life's greatest experiences are just on the other side of fear.

I challenge you to start with something small. Look around for existing needs in your community and organizations that are helping meet those needs. Find an organization doing good work and partner with them. Plan to regularly volunteer along with your family or friends. When you're finished volunteering, go out for ice cream and celebrate that you did something meaningful together. These opportunities can create great memories and will also help reinforce important values which you and your friends/family will carry for the rest of your lives.

Becoming Mission Minded: Where is a place where you can volunteer along with your family and friends to make an impact in your community? Don't be afraid to step out of your comfort zone and make the leap!

Authors Note: My youngest daughter Mallory, who is wired a lot like me when it comes to adventure, made me promise I would take her skydiving when she was old enough. Saturday,

May 9, 2020, I kept my promise. For the second time in less than a year, we loaded the family in the car and headed to Falcon Skydiving. This time it was me, Mallory and Mycah's boyfriend, Brendan Norwine, who made the jump. Knowing what to expect made skydiving a little easier the second time, but it was still a scary experience. Once again, we enjoyed a day filled with great stories, lasting memories and lots of laughs. On May 27, 2022 Brendan and Mycah got married, so currently I've been skydiving with four of my five children. Kyndal, your father-in-law is still waiting to take you on a date to Falcon Skydiving.

8

Moon Shine

"A tree is known by its fruit, a man by his deeds. A good deed is never lost, he who sows courtesy reaps friendship, and he who plants kindness gathers love." - Saint Basil

UrbanDictionary.com defines 'Outkicking Your Coverage' as *to engage in a romantic relationship with a person who is much better looking, and/or smarter, and/or in a higher socioeconomic class than you. Essentially, a person who is widely considered to be 'out of your league.'* For anyone who has ever met my wife Cam, it's easy to see who got the better end of the deal. When Cam said, "I do," I felt like I had become the president of the 'Outkicked Your Coverage' club.

I have always heard opposites attract, and I quickly learned this was true in our marriage. During premarital counseling our pastor shared three things couples fight most about in marriage: money, sex and in-laws. Well, I have always gotten along great with my in-laws, and Cam and I both agree sex is a lot of fun (I include this in the book just to embarrass my children).

Money, however, is a different story. When it comes to finances, Cam and I definitely do not see eye to eye. I like to think of myself as fiscally conservative. My beautiful wife has a different name for it. She calls it being a 'tightwad.' I believe that is a Latin word for a man who doesn't like to part easily with his hard-earned money. It didn't take us long to discover marriage came with a few challenges, and I had a lot to learn about women.

I grew up with two brothers. Other than my mom, females were totally absent in our home. My brothers and I were clueless when it came to understanding why girls thought and acted the way they did. One of the things which completely dumbfounded me after getting married was why my wife, who had two feet just like me, needed so many different pairs of shoes. To this day it still doesn't make sense to my male brain. Each time I walk into our bedroom closet and look at the shoe rack I feel like I'm married to a centipede.

One day early in my marriage I was unable to hide my frustration; I made the mistake of telling my wife buying so many pairs of shoes was a waste of money. I quickly learned that making a comment about her shoe collection was a great way to create a major conflict in our new marriage. What I perceived as a waste of money, she viewed as a necessity. My careless and clueless comment made for a very long evening in a very small apartment. Even though Cam has attempted to explain it to me several times, I still have never understood why girls need so many pairs of shoes. However, I now fully understand if I want to live with a happy wife there better be money set aside for shoes in our budget.

Another of the important lessons marriage has taught me is I don't like conflict, and I definitely don't like drama. Thankfully Cam doesn't like them either. I have been around some people who seem to thrive on conflict. They always have a scowl on their face as if someone peed on their breakfast cereal. I have a difficult time being around these people because I feel like I'm walking on eggshells. If you slip up and happen to say the wrong thing at the wrong time it sets them off with an angry outburst. This is not what Cam and I want for our marriage.

We want our marriage and our home to be a warm and happy place that's receptive to changes. Early on I discovered

I needed to become more generous, kinder, and I needed to learn to look for the funny in situations. As I worked on these areas my life became much more enjoyable. I found my personal life, as well as my work life, became much more meaningful and joyful when I focused on kindness, generosity and reacting with humor.

Cam and I like volunteering with organizations who are impacting the lives of others. One of those organizations is the Tim Tebow Foundation. One night every year more than 600 churches from around the world host special prom events honoring young adults with special needs and disabilities. The event is called Night to Shine, and it was created by former NFL quarterback Tim Tebow. Although Tim is a former quarterback for the Denver Broncos, which is one of the Chiefs biggest rivals, I have a tremendous amount of respect for him. Regardless of what sport people play or which team they play for, I respect any athlete willing to use his or her platform to make a positive impact in the lives of others.

I was told my first Night to Shine prom would be an unforgettable experience, and it did not disappoint. In Kansas City, a large number of churches come together to host Night to Shine at Arrowhead Stadium. One of the organizers asked if KC Wolf could make an appearance, and since KC Wolf lived in my garage, I told him there was a very good chance KC Wolf could attend that evening. I had previously worked with Special Olympics and several other special needs groups, and I knew it would be a fun time.

Since it was a prom event, I vowed to be the best looking prom goer and dressed KC Wolf up in a tuxedo. My job was to escort the prom guests into Arrowhead. While KC Wolf pushed wheelchairs and assisted those with handicaps, the other volunteers stood in two lines across from each other and cheered for the special guests as I escorted them in. You could tell by the smiles this was going to be a special evening for everyone. After all the guests arrived, I went inside and spent the rest of the night posing for pictures, entertaining folks and groovin' to the music. There was no shortage of dance partners for KC Wolf on the dance floor on this special evening, but I wasn't the only one bustin' a move. I was very impressed with all the volunteers who were out dancing with the special guests. The Night to Shine volunteers were extremely generous with their time, sacrificing their entire night to help make the evening a huge success. Everyone walked away feeling good, knowing it was time well spent.

Over the years I have volunteered with many different organizations around the Kansas City area. I've discovered some of the happiest people in our city are also some of the kindest. This is no surprise because my parents have always taught me the principle–you reap what you sow. Sow kindness, reap kindness. Sow joy and happiness, reap joy and happiness. Not only are the kindest people the happiest people, they also seem to be the ones making the greatest impact with their lives.

I want kindness to be one of the character qualities people see in me. Whether or not I'm dressed in costume, I want people to walk away from an encounter with me saying, "Dan is a very kind man." I can tell I must be getting older and more mature because in my youth, I was definitely more concerned with being cool than being kind. I'm now at a stage in my life where kindness is more important to me than being cool. I want my life to make a difference in this world, so I look for opportunities throughout my day to do kind things for others. When I become intentional and start looking around, I am amazed at all the opportunities I have each day to make a difference.

One day on my way back to Arrowhead from a KC Wolf appearance I pulled up to a stoplight. There was a homeless man standing on the corner with a cardboard sign. I rolled down my window, smiled at him and asked if he wanted to go to lunch. He said yes, and I told him to meet me across the street at Taco Bell. Ten minutes later, my new friend and I were eating tacos and enjoying lunch together. I enjoyed getting to know him and listening to his story. We knew many of the same people at the Kansas City Rescue Mission homeless shelter. When lunch was over, I thanked him for dining with me and handed him a few dollars so he could take the bus back to the rescue mission for the night. As he walked away, I said a short prayer asking God to bless my new friend. Taking him to lunch had cost me a little bit of time and money, but it was worth every penny because we both walked away encouraged. Leaving Taco Bell I was reminded we all make mistakes in life, but just because someone makes a bad choice doesn't necessarily mean they're a bad person. I know I make my share of mistakes every single day.

A short time later I met some other good people who had made bad choices when I had the opportunity to speak to the inmates at the Kansas Juvenile Correctional Complex in Topeka, KS. As expected, security was extremely tight, but after a thorough search of my bag the prison guards let me bring in my KC Wolf costume. Although I wasn't allowed to wear it inside the prison, I showed the inmates my costume and spent 45 minutes telling them about my career and answering questions. Throughout the evening I tried to shower them with kindness and words of encouragement. I discovered the inmates are just like kids. If you make them laugh and demonstrate to them that you truly care, they will listen to what you say. I challenged them to look for ways to make positive changes each day so they would be ready to succeed when they returned to life outside of prison.

The feeling I receive from showing kindness to others has become addicting. One benefit I noticed when starting to demonstrate more kindness in my marriage and in my other relationships was a major reduction in conflict and drama. Being kind reminds me of Chamois Butter. In the summer of 2017, I talked my brother Dave into joining me on the Bike Across Kansas (BAK). BAK is an annual eight-day bicycle tour across the state of Kansas, which started in 1975 to promote health and wellness and introduce people to the history and beauty of the state.

Even though my brother and I own bikes, we aren't exactly what you would call road warriors. We casually trained for about six weeks and then just prayed we would survive it. We started the week by taking a picture together at the Colorado/Kansas border. Eight days later two very weary and sore brothers posed for another photo, this time dipping our bike tires into the Missouri River in Kansas City. During the trip, I pedaled 549 miles. As expected, the body part which hurt the worst at the end of BAK was the body part at the end of my back. Yes, my rear end. Every part of my body which touched or rubbed against my bike seat while I pedaled was chafed and hurting.

Thankfully, before our trip a friend of mine had told us about Chamois Butter. In the biking world, Chamois Butter is better known as 'Butt Butter.' My friend described Chamois Butter as a really thick lotion applied to your crotch area to help reduce friction. Reducing friction helps create a much more pleasant bike ride. As I think back on our Bike Across Kansas, I'm reminded kindness is a lot like Butt Butter. When I'm smart enough to apply a little kindness each day, it helps reduce friction and makes my ride through life much more enjoyable. When I get in the habit of applying a little kindness in my relationships at home, in my workplace and in my world, it makes me a better person. It also reduces drama and allows me to have a more positive impact on the lives of those around me.

Being generous and kind has helped improve my relationships, but what has significantly increased my laughter and joy in life is when I began to slow down and look for the funny in every situation. Like many men, there are times I allow myself to get too busy. Busyness always robs my joy because I start living for the urgent instead of the important things in life. When I get too busy, people and projects are no longer enjoyable. Everything becomes an item I just try to get checked off my to-do list.

I realize this is not a good way to treat myself and others. When my priorities get out of line, my life is miserable. Just like I don't like conflict and drama, I also don't enjoy misery. I've learned the best way for me to avoid misery is to slow down and enjoy the journey. When I slow down and start looking for the funny in situations, my perspective changes.

Situations that would have upset me in the past now make me laugh. A good example is an appearance I made at a Burger King in Belton, MO. The manager invited KC Wolf to come out on a Saturday morning to help their store celebrate the kickoff to the Chiefs season. Fast food appearances are always fun because lots of people circulate through these restaurants throughout the day. I arrived early and changed into my costume in the storage closet. After making my grand entrance and entertaining the customers inside the store, I went outside along the street to wave at cars and try to attract more business. Many of the cars drove by honking their horns and yelling "Go Chiefs," and I passed the time counting how many cars I could get to blow their horns.

Just as I was about to go back inside the restaurant I heard a guy yell, "Hey KC Wolf." When I turned to look, I saw a sports car with two college kids inside. The driver proceeded to salute me with his tallest finger while his friend in the passenger seat dropped his pants and mooned me out the car window. All I could see through my fur was two white buns shining in the sunlight. I could hear them laughing as they drove away. My first reaction was to get upset, but instead I decided if this young man was going to go to that much trouble to show off his rear end, I might as well laugh too. KC Wolf waved to them with one hand and acted like he was covering up his eyes with the other. When I arrived home and told Cam she also got a good chuckle from my experience. I soon discovered the more I started to look for the funny in life, more funny things began to happen.

Another memorable moment happened not too long after my incident at Burger King. I was invited to speak at a small elementary school in north central Kansas. Cawker City is one of several places claiming to be the home of the world's largest ball of twine. Each year a twine-a-thon is held in August to increase the size of the ball. I had been to Cawker City one other time with my dad, but this time I was on my own. As I drove into Cawker City I stopped so I could get an updated picture of KC Wolf in front of the ball of twine. I'm not sure why I felt a need to stop because KC Wolf never ages. Although I look and feel older out of costume, KC Wolf looks the same as he did the first time I got my picture with the ball of twine years earlier.

The town is so small it's always difficult finding someone to take a picture. After a nice lady stopped and helped me, I got back in my car and drove a few more blocks to the elementary school. The principal escorted me to the cafeteria, where I set up my equipment in front of the stage. I then went into a back room to change. As the kids entered the room, KC Wolf came out to greet them at the door. After the principal introduced me, I took off the costume and introduced myself to the students. After showing a short mascot highlight video, I spent about 20 minutes talking with the students about showing respect for others and not being bullies. When I finished speaking, I saved 10 minutes for a Q & A time.

The students asked several good questions, and then one of the older boys asked if he could try on the costume. I smiled and invited him to come on up. When he got to the front, I noticed there wasn't going to be enough space between me and the first row of children to dress him up in the costume. I asked the principal if it would be okay to dress him up on the stage. As the principal opened the curtain on the stage, the students started snickering and laughing out loud. I watched as the teachers tried not to laugh.

When I turned around to see what was so funny, once again there was a naked butt in front of me. Apparently, the health teacher had placed a naked mannequin behind the stage earlier in the day and had failed to tell the staff. I couldn't stop laughing as the principal scrambled to find a towel to cover up the naked buns. After the assembly was over the principal kept apologizing, but I told him I actually wanted to thank him because I knew I would laugh about that school assembly for the rest of my life.

One of the things I really enjoy about working as KC Wolf is getting to visit small towns like Cawker City throughout the Midwest. Most of the folks I meet in these small towns are kind and down to earth. I've enjoyed many laughs during my travels. I especially enjoy reading the creative messages and signs posted in front of churches, schools and local businesses. The small town of Eldon, MO has been a favorite, and I always make time to visit the donut shop there because they post humorous messages on their sign out front. The first time I saw their sign I had to turn around and take a picture. It read "MY STOMACH IS FLAT BUT THE 'L' IS SILENT." I not only laughed at the message, but I also laughed at the fact it was appropriately displayed in front of a donut shop. A month later I drove through Eldon again, and the sign said "I LOVE EATING MY CHILDREN & NOT USING COMMAS." I had to read it several times before I understood the message. Once it sank in, I got another good laugh. If you look for the funny in life, there is plenty to be found.

Cam and I have been married for more than a quarter of a century. I still don't fully understand why she needs so many shoes. However, I'm thankful for the lessons those shoes and my marriage have taught me, important life lessons about how to get along with others and living a life of influence. I've learned generous people are always happier than selfish people. Kind people always have a more lasting impact on the lives of others than cool people. Finally, I can promise when you begin to look for the funny in every situation, your journey through life will be much more enjoyable.

Becoming Mission Minded: What is something kind you can do for your spouse today? Are you considered a tightwad? Could you begin to spend a little more time, energy and money on your spouse? Try it out; I think you will enjoy the long-term dividends.

9

Where My Passion For Orphans Began

"Those who give much without sacrifice are reckoned as having given little." - Erwin Lutzer

One benefit of being a mascot for so many years is I have become really good at nonverbal communication. When I first started being a mascot back in college, I learned mascots are not supposed to talk. When a mascot speaks in costume it ruins the mascot magic. Even though adults understand mascots are just people dressed up in costumes, this is not always the case for children. For kids, there is something magical about a life-size stuffed animal walking around.

Walt Disney understood this concept, and it is one of the reasons Disney's Magic Kingdom continues to make millions and millions of dollars each year. We took several family vacations to Disney when my kids were young. I always left Magic Kingdom both impressed and depressed; I was impressed by the magic Mickey Mouse and the other Disney characters created not only for my kids but for children from all over the world, but I was also depressed because each time I left a Disney theme park, money had magically disappeared from my wallet. Mickey Mouse knows how to get your cash.

Although many Disney characters have voices, most sports mascots do not. The three characters I have portrayed over the years (Truman Tiger, Fredbird and KC Wolf) are all non-speaking mascots. When you are not allowed to use your voice, it forces you to learn how to communicate using only your actions. These nonverbal skills come in handy when I take KC Wolf on overseas mission trips. I have discovered I can communicate with people in any language as long as I'm dressed up as KC Wolf. However, once I take the costume off, I desperately need an interpreter.

My first overseas mission trip in June 2014 didn't include KC Wolf. I served as an adult sponsor with our church youth group from Lee's Summit Community Church. We took a trip to work at an orphanage in Honduras, and God used this trip to stir a passion in me for orphans around the world.

I was not able to bring KC Wolf along on the trip because I was still recovering from the bungee jump accident in November 2013. I have never really liked calling it an accident, because I believe there are no such thing as accidents; they are all just incidents in God's perfect plan for my life. God used my Honduras trip to change me and to give me a new perspective and purpose.

In the five months leading up to the trip, I spent countless hours doing very painful therapy and rehabilitation. Due to my injuries, I couldn't work so I spent lots of time at home and with my physical therapist (aka physical terrorist). As much as I hate to admit it, I became really good at throwing pity parties for myself and secretly hoping others would join me. I discovered when I spent all my time at home, I lived in a very small world, and while living in that small world my problems all seemed huge.

During my trip to Honduras, however, God opened my eyes and showed me I live in a big, big world. As I began to look around and see others living in this big world with me, it began to put my own problems into perspective. I realized there were many people in this world who were far worse off than me, and they weren't sitting around throwing pity parties for themselves.

I remember standing in the gated courtyard of the Yo Quiero Ser orphanage in San Pedro Sula, Honduras. I was surrounded by dirt, chickens and a group of smiling orphans in ragged clothing. As I stood watching the orphans play, I was convicted of my own self-centeredness. I fought back tears and quietly asked God to forgive me for taking my many blessings for granted. I had wallowed in self-pity with my focus on myself for long enough. I knew it was time for an attitude adjustment. It was time to shift my focus. I had always enjoyed working with kids, but this trip to Honduras stirred in my heart a love and passion for helping orphans, widows and the poor around the world. Serving in Honduras also taught me another valuable lesson.

One of the service projects we worked on in Honduras was digging a hole 10 feet long x 10 feet wide x 10 feet deep. The hole was going to be used as a community septic tank. As we worked many hours out in the hot sun, I quickly realized helping others isn't always glamorous work. Most of the time it requires tremendous sacrifice.

Two years after my trip to Honduras, KC Wolf joined me for the first time ever on a mission trip to Haiti. I was excited to see how the orphans would respond, and I was also excited because my oldest daughter Mycah would be joining me. My dear friend and longtime accountability partner Rod Handley, along with his two sons and three other college age students, were also part of our team. Our destination was the city of Limbe in the northern district of Haiti.

Most people who travel to Haiti fly into Port-Au-Prince, but we flew into the northern city of Cap Haitian. Traveling with KC Wolf is always an adventure, even when traveling in the United States, but going into Haiti proved to be memorable. Since the extra-large costume bag KC Wolf travels in doesn't look like any of the other suitcases at the airport, people are naturally curious about what is inside my huge bag. If they get really close, I'm sure it smells like I'm transporting a dead body. I assure them it's only a musty mascot costume.

Since it was my first trip with KC Wolf to a third world country, I wasn't sure what to expect. After landing, we grabbed our luggage and proceeded to customs. I had been warned it could take hours and perhaps my costume might not be allowed to enter the country. I couldn't keep from laughing as I watched the customs agent unzip my mascot bag. His eyes got as big as saucers, and he quickly zipped the bag back up and told me to move on. I would love to have known what was going through his mind, because he acted like he had just seen the world's largest Voodoo doll.

After clearing customs in record time we carried our bags outside into the stifling heat and humidity. We loaded our luggage onto the back of a small pickup truck, climbed into the bed of the truck and began what was the longest, bumpiest and dirtiest two hour ride I had ever taken.

Although Grace Mission orphanage is only 15 miles from the airport, I quickly learned the roads in Haiti are nothing like the roads in the United States. Haiti is perhaps the poorest nation in the Western Hemisphere. It was obvious they spend very little money on their roads. I had never seen or experienced potholes so large. I was also astonished by the amount of trash sitting along the side of the road. We learned there are no garbage trucks in the area to collect trash, so most Haitians throw their trash into the trench which runs along the side of the road. Then they just wait for the heavy rains to come and wash the trash down the trench, straight into the ocean. Haiti is a beautiful country, but unfortunately the roadways, ocean front and beaches are filled with garbage.

As we weaved our way down the road trying to avoid hitting the massive potholes and people, I noticed a motorcycle racing past us carrying four passengers and a driver. I had never seen five people on one motorcycle. Apparently, they weren't too concerned about safety because the driver was the only one wearing a helmet. Things were already getting interesting!

Thirty smiling orphans greeted us when we arrived at the orphanage. They were anxious to start playing with their new American guests. We quickly learned the boys' favorite games included soccer, basketball and marbles. The girls loved to braid hair. Since my daughter Mycah has long hair, she was very popular with all the little girls. We spent our first afternoon playing lots of games and getting to know the kids. Late in the afternoon the children gathered in the cafeteria for dinner, while we ate in a much quieter room with the orphanage directors.

Ray and Bonnie VanSlyke have served as the directors at Grace Mission orphanage since 2007. During dinner the VanSlykes told us their story of how God called them to minister to orphans in Haiti. They shared the difficulties of trying to run an orphanage in a third world country, along with the challenges of trying to successfully love and parent 30 orphans from ages 2–18.

Early in their ministry, they realized it was going to be impossible to do all the work themselves, so they trained a Haitian staff to help care for the children. The staff keep the orphanage clean, cook healthy food, discipline adequately, teach the children Godly principles and maintain general order. After nine years there were (and still are) plenty of challenges, but there was no doubt the VanSlykes had an organized system in place which was working well.

It was clear Ray and Bonnie loved the orphans. It was also obvious the orphans loved them as well. As I listened to their story I couldn't help but admire them for the sacrifices they had made. They left a comfortable life in the United States to move to Haiti so they could make a difference in the lives of orphans. People like them inspire and challenge me.

After dinner the children knew the routine. They headed for their rooms to brush their teeth and get ready for bed. Our group stayed in the dining room and played cards until the lights went out. Every evening around 9:00 p.m. the power turns off in Haiti, and everything goes dark. We had been warned, so each of us had a flashlight to help us find our way back to our rooms. Since it was extremely hot and there was no air conditioning, we used our flashlights to take cold showers just before going to bed. The bunk beds were covered by mosquito nets. The goal was to climb in bed and fall asleep before sweating again. Falling asleep was also a challenge because of the beating of the Voodoo drums in the distance.

Another thing I learned on this trip was the Haitian people don't like to sleep in. The country turns the electricity back on before 5:00 a.m. and people are stirring around well before the sun comes up. Therefore, we were always out of bed by 6:00 a.m. at the latest, which you may recall from Chapter 2 is way too early for me.

After breakfast, the kids at the orphanage do their daily chores and school work before they are allowed to go out and play. On my second day at the orphanage I figured it was a good time to introduce the kids to KC Wolf. I went back to my room and put on the costume. When KC Wolf came dancing into the courtyard where the kids were gathered it was fantastic watching their reactions and listening to their screams of delight. Clearly the kids had never seen anything like it before in their lives. I spent around 30 minutes out in the hot sun getting pictures and playing with the orphans before I finally sneaked back to my room to take off the costume and get a drink. My body wasn't used to performing in temperatures quite so extreme. I was soaked in sweat. I hung the Wolf suit up to dry in my room and went back outside dressed as myself. It was fun watching the older kids trying to figure out which of the Americans had been dressed in the crazy costume. The next day KC Wolf made another surprise appearance, which once again created lots of excitement.

What really impressed me about Grace Mission was the fact they not only minister to orphans, but they also have a senior adult home housing several widows from the community. After entertaining at the orphanage, KC Wolf visited the senior adults. Once again it was very evident that no matter their age, the Haitian people were not used to having mascots visit their country. As I looked through fur at the faces of the widows, I could tell they were enjoying the moment by their toothless grins. They didn't have a lot of teeth, but the few teeth they did have were showing. They were some of the most beautiful smiles I have ever seen. There is no better feeling than knowing what you are doing is helping to bring joy and happiness to someone else's life.

On day four of our trip we gathered all the children into the school area and KC Wolf made another appearance. However, this time I took the costume off and revealed to the children who was under the suit. Most of them already suspected it was "Mr. Dan" in the costume. Since I had my computer and a projector on the trip, I was able to share with the kids the same KC Wolf highlight video I show to students in the United States. I did a short program with the kids, answering their questions and showing them the individual KC Wolf costume parts.

We attempted to have one of the orphans try the costume on, but his legs were very short, and KC Wolf's belly rested on the ground. He looked more like a Hershey's Kiss than an overweight wolf with legs and tennis shoes. Needless to say, it brought many laughs. My favorite part of the program was at the end when I had the chance to encourage and pray for the kids. In the Bible, the book of Proverbs talks about the power of the tongue. It says, "Words kill, words give life; they're either poison or fruit—you choose" (Proverbs 18:21, MSG).

Whenever I have the opportunity to share with young people, my goal is to speak life into them. Whether I'm speaking to kids in the United States or speaking through a translator in a foreign country, I want my words to be an encouragement to those who listen. My prayer is for children to walk away knowing they are special and loved by God and me. My good friend Joe Calhoon once told me, "You can be a wind in someone's sail, or you can be an anchor in their tail." Joe is exactly right. Your words can be used to encourage or discourage others. I want to speak life and love every opportunity I can.

After speaking to the children at the orphanage, we presented a KC Wolf program for the widows. They enjoyed it as much as the children. Instead of trying on the entire costume though, the widows just wanted to try on the KC Wolf head. Once again, I was reminded that most adults are big kids trapped in older bodies.

One of the things I noticed at Grace Mission was the widows at the senior adult house didn't have much to do other than sit and watch the children play in the courtyard. One afternoon I found some lumber in a shed and decided to make the seniors a Washers game. Washers is a game my family plays a lot during summer vacations when we go to our lake house. It basically consists of two short wooden boxes with a can attached to the middle of each box. The boxes are placed about 12 feet apart, and you attempt to throw washers into the can. If your washer lands in the can you get three points. If it lands in the box you score one point. The first player to score 21 points is the winner. Trying to explain to the senior adults how to play was quite challenging, since the only language they spoke was Creole and the only language I spoke was English. After several practice rounds they finally caught on to how to play. Once again their toothless grins revealed their excitement about this new game. As I sat back and listened to them cheer for each other when an occasional washer landed in the box, I realized it doesn't take a lot of money to be a blessing to others. We had taken some old lumber and a couple of cans and turned it into an afternoon of fun and laughs. Playing Washers with widows in Haiti is a memory I will forever cherish.

Saturdays are lively days in the city of Limbe. There was a weekend festival being held on the riverbank on the outskirts of town, and many of the local residents gathered there to celebrate. Ray VanSlyke kept a four-wheeler at Grace Mission which he used as a work vehicle and for making trips into town. He thought it would be fun to have KC Wolf make a surprise appearance at the festival by riding in on the back of the four-wheeler. He wanted to watch the reaction on the faces of the Haitian people who weren't used to seeing mascots. He asked Jacquelin, a young Haitian man who worked at Grace Mission, if he would take me to the festival. While the rest of our team loaded into the bed of Ray's pickup truck, I put on my costume and jumped onto the back of the four-wheeler. Since I didn't know my way around town, I was happy to let Jacquelin do the driving while I sat on the back of the four-wheeler waving to the crowd. When we arrived at the riverbank, the scene looked like a Chiefs tailgate party. Everyone was eating, drinking and listening to loud music, and it didn't take long for people to notice the large costumed character who had arrived at the party. A group of excited kids started running behind us, yelling and laughing. When we got to the area where the DJ was blasting his music, I jumped off the four-wheeler and started dancing. I quickly learned that Haitians love to dance. So many people started to crowd around me it felt like I was in the middle of a mosh pit. I tried to stay close to the four-wheeler just in case things got too crazy and we needed to make a quick exit. After dancing to several unfamiliar songs and taking numerous photos with the excited crowd, I jumped back onto the four-wheeler and Jacquelin drove me back to Grace Mission for a much-needed water break. In all the appearance lasted less than 45 minutes. I was very glad Ray had suggested the idea because I was able to experience a little taste of the Haitian culture, and I know KC Wolf added a lot of excitement to the festival.

Another highlight during my trip to Haiti was getting to preach at the local church on Sunday morning. I have talked at many churches in my life, but once again what made this opportunity both exciting and frightening was only a few of the members understood English. Thankfully there was an interpreter who translated my message. After the Sunday sermon the pastor asked if I would put on the costume so the church members could get their pictures taken with KC Wolf. I went back to my room, changed quickly and spent the next 45 minutes getting photos with church members of all ages.

The day before our departure, we took a number of the orphans on a hike up to a beautiful waterfall. Our goal was to enjoy a day filled with fun and laughter, a day the orphans would remember long after we were gone. As we walked up the mountain to the waterfall, one of the little girls started to feel sick. Derek Handley, Rod's oldest son, offered to carry her. I was impressed with his willingness to help because the path up to the waterfall was not an easy climb and she wasn't a small girl. Derek not only carried her to the waterfall, but he also carried her back down as well. It was encouraging to watch Derek and the other college students from our team going out of their way to make the orphans feel loved. We didn't realize it at the time, but Derek's offer to help that day would end up being a huge sacrifice. It resulted in him also getting very sick. After returning home to Kansas City, Derek was hospitalized for over a week with viral meningitis.

I know God works in mysterious ways, and this was definitely the case following Derek's illness. Because of Derek's lengthy hospital stay, the Handley family met their insurance deductible for the year. As a result, later that year Rod scheduled a medical procedure which he wouldn't have scheduled otherwise due to the cost. It revealed he had stage four cancer. The doctors went in and removed eight cancerous tumors from his body. Today Rod is cancer free. God took what appeared to be a bad situation and through an amazing sequence of events used it to bring healing to my friend Rod. Coincidence? I think not.

The hardest thing about traveling to Limbe was saying goodbye. When our team arrived we were complete strangers, but by the end of the week we had developed many close friendships. I was amazed how attached I had become to many of the orphans and widows after spending one short week together. My trip to Haiti also gave me a whole new appreciation for my air conditioned home in Kansas City where I could stay cool and shower with warm water.

Before departing the Cap Haitian airport on our flight back to the United States, I thought about the sacrifices our team made to visit the Grace Mission orphanage. The trip had personally cost me vacation time, money, energy and comfort, but it was well worth it. Compared to Ray and Bonnie VanSlyke, my sacrifice seemed insignificant. This trip to Haiti taught me that even my seemingly small sacrifices can make a big impact in the lives of others if I do it with love. Stephen Covey once said, "Love is a verb. Love is something you do, the sacrifices you make, the giving of self. If you want to study love, study those who sacrifice for others. Love–the feeling–is a fruit of love, the verb." Ray, Bonnie and the other workers who daily make sacrifices for the orphans and widows at Grace Mission are a great example to me of what true love really looks like.

Love means action. Love means rolling up my sleeves, getting dirty and getting involved. I knew this trip would be the first of many for KC Wolf to visit orphanages around the world, and the Chiefs organization and the Hunt family are very supportive of my work with orphans. I'm committed to using my platform as an NFL mascot to put love into action. God gave me a passion for helping orphans and widows. This passion continued to grow with every orphan I met in Haiti. I know I will never again be content standing on the sidelines as a spectator. I want to be in the game and be part of the action. I know it will require sacrifice, but I pray God gives me more and more opportunities to show love to those who desperately need it most. I want to use the KC Wolf costume to do more than just entertain fans at football games. My desire is to use it to continue to bring joy to orphans and widows around the globe.

Becoming Mission Minded: Love is a verb. What small sacrifice or action can you make today to show love to someone in this world?

10

Rice, Rice and More Rice

"Everyone has baggage; maybe we should help each other carry it."
- Rob Liano

My wife and I have the privilege of helping support numerous organizations and ministries around the world who are making a big impact in the lives of the poor and needy. One of those organizations is Reliant Ministries, which has developed a micro loan program at several churches in the Philippines. Reliant provides small, no interest loans to people so they can purchase items or equipment to help start up small businesses. Once the business is up and running, they slowly pay back the loan amount. This allows Reliant to take the money and make other small loans to other individuals in the community.

It is always rewarding to receive thank you letters from Reliant telling us how our donation has been utilized. One lady was excited to learn she was getting a loan to help her purchase a sewing machine. She used the sewing machine to make small hand towels which she then sold in her community to help support her family. What Cam and I love about Reliant is they are a ministry who believes in giving people a hand up instead of a handout.

In the spring of 2017 we received a letter from Reliant telling us about their work in the Philippines. Pastor Mike Bergen is a longtime friend who has worked with Reliant in the Philippines for many years. Mike mentioned he had talked with several pastors in the Philippines who wanted to provide several women's conferences for the ladies in their churches.

The pastors explained how the women work very hard but are greatly underappreciated in their communities. These pastors wanted to encourage these women and thank them for their contributions. Mike mentioned he was hoping to gather a group of American women who would be willing to travel to the Philippines and speak at the conferences.

As soon as I read the letter, I knew Cam would be a perfect fit for the trip. Cam is a licensed marriage and family therapist. Even though she would never admit it, she is also an excellent speaker. Over the years Cam has presented at several women's conferences. I knew speaking in the Philippines with the help of an interpreter would be out of Cam's comfort zone, but I also knew she would do a terrific job. It took a little convincing, but Cam finally agreed.

I called Mike and asked if both Cam and I could join him on the trip. He was not only thrilled Cam had agreed to speak, but also my presence meant he wouldn't be the only male going on the trip. Mike asked if I could bring along KC Wolf and speak at several of the local schools while the female speakers were presenting at the conferences. Once again, talking to kids in a foreign country who don't speak my language sounded like an adventure. I was ready for another exciting opportunity, especially with Cam joining me.

The day we left for the Philippines, Cam and I crawled out of our bed at 2:30 a.m. to get to the airport in time for our early flight. Approximately 34 hours later we crawled back into a bed at the Sleep Well hotel in San Jose Del Monte, Philippines. Even though the hotel was far from luxurious, we were so exhausted from traveling that we slept great.

We woke up around 9:00 a.m. to the sound of honking horns and traffic. Our hotel sat on one of the busy streets leading up to the market in an area of the city known as Sampang Palay. The streets were filled with motorcycles, bicycles and cars, but the most popular means of transportation was Jeepneys. These vehicles resembled buses with crowded seating, each painted in bright colors with festive decorations representing the Philippine culture.

Our team decided to meet in the hotel lobby at 10:00 a.m. to grab a bite to eat. Our group from the United States consisted of five people: Cam, me, Mike Bergen and two other ladies named Nancy and Dawn, who had traveled along to help with the women's conferences.

We walked to the market and ate breakfast at a fast food restaurant called Jollibee. Jollibee is similar to McDonald's. They have many locations throughout the country, and there are always long lines of people waiting to eat. The biggest difference between Jollibee and McDonald's is that almost every menu item at Jollibee includes rice. I didn't realize it at the time, but this meal was the beginning of the longest rice eating streak of my life. For the next eight days I ate rice at every meal. During the trip I ate a wide variety of fruits, vegetables and meats, but the one constant at every meal was rice. Eating large amounts of white rice is hard on a man's digestive system. By midweek I was wishing I had packed a box of Fiber One bars for the trip.

After breakfast we walked back to the hotel, where we met our driver for the week. Danny De La Cruz pastors a small church in an area called San Vincente, but during the week he works as a Jeepney driver. Danny is a jokester who loves to laugh. He has a big smile and a tremendous personality to boot. Right away I knew Danny and I were going to get along really well. Thankfully Danny spoke English much better than I spoke Tagalog, the primary language in the Philippines. Even though I understood most of what Danny said, there were several other times when I just had to smile and nod my head because I didn't have a clue as to what he was saying.

Danny drove us to meet Ed Samontanes, who worked in construction but also pastored a small church in the area. His church consisted of a room that could seat approximately 35 people. He said if you arrived for church early you could probably get a seat, but if you showed up late you would have to stand or listen to the service from outside the building. Cam and I chuckled because we realized if our church back in Kansas City was similarly sized we would be standing at church every single Sunday.

Pastor Ed and his wife, Sister Lucy, showed us around the community and introduced us to several shop owners who were part of the microloan program. It was encouraging to hear firsthand the impact the microloan program was having on the lives of people far away from my home in Kansas City.

What really struck me was the amount of time, love and effort Ed and Lucy were investing in helping others in their circle of influence. Even though Ed worked full time in construction and Lucy stayed busy taking care of the family, they still found time to minister to others. They had recently helped build a church in the small mountain village of San Mateo, which was located over an hour away from their home. Every week they would make the long and bumpy drive up the mountain to minister to the villagers. Sister Lucy and Ed raised money to purchase flip flops they distributed to the children of San Mateo, because many of them often went without shoes. They agreed to take us to see the new church in San Mateo later during our trip.

We spent the remainder of the day getting to know our new friends and meeting other pastors in San Jose Del Monte. Pastor German Arce is the president of the Independent Churches of Great Commission in the Philippines. He invited us over to his house for dinner that evening. We met his wife Joy and their two children, Irish and Herschel. We also enjoyed a delicious meal which, of course, included more rice.

The next morning after eating another high carb breakfast at Jollibee's, we traveled to the first women's conference. Since hosting a conference for women had never been done before, the pastors were unsure what kind of turnout they would get. Although it was scheduled to start at 10:00 a.m. we quickly found out nothing really begins on time in the Philippines. Nobody appeared too stressed when 10:00 a.m. rolled around and there were only five women in attendance. Danny assured me the women would start showing up soon. Sure enough, 20 minutes later the room was starting to fill up. When the conference finally began around 10:30 a.m. I counted 72 women of all ages. They were nicely dressed and looked excited about participating in the conference. Pastor Arce was thrilled to see so many women there.

While Cam, Nancy and Dawn spent the day at the conference, Mike and I rode along with Danny and pastor Jojo Cabanding. Like many of the other pastors, Jojo also worked a second job. He helped run the Hanniah Learning Home, which was a school in an area of the city known as Harmony. I was eager to connect with Pastor Jojo because he had invited me to preach at his church on Sunday morning. He asked if I could start off dressed as KC Wolf and then take off the costume to deliver the message. He was thrilled about the possibility of having KC Wolf be part of the service. He knew the children would be excited when they saw a mascot running around at church. I had preached at many churches in the United States and also in Haiti, so I figured speaking at a church in the Philippines would be fun as well.

While visiting with Pastor Jojo about the Sunday service, Danny drove us to San Roque where we met with another group of pastors. Pastor Francis Olaes and Pastor Nato Adaya were making final preparations to pack up their belongings and move their families to Cambodia. They were honoring

God's call to leave their homes, learn a new language and move to another country.

I was challenged by the faith of these men. These two families didn't have much at all, but what they did have they were willing to give up in order to go and help others who had even less. They were leaving a place comfortable to them in order to make a difference in the lives of people who were even worse off. I wondered if I would be willing to make a similar sacrifice. I was deeply touched and challenged by my new Philippine pastor friends. They were some of the most unselfish men I had ever met.

After our meeting we drove back to get the ladies from the conference, and then we all went out for another meal filled with white rice and chicken. The best part of the meal was a dessert called Halo Halo. The menu described it as 'the ultimate summertime treat,' a layered dessert consisting of sweetened beans, fruits and shaved ice drizzled with evaporated milk and ice cream. Since it was extremely hot, the ice cream sounded really good. I decided adding some high fiber beans and fruit into my diet would also be good for my digestive system. After finishing that ultimate summertime treat, we headed back to the hotel. My favorite part about the Sleep Well hotel was our room was air conditioned. As a result, I indeed slept well almost every night.

Sunday morning Danny dropped Cam and I off at Pastor Jojo's church in Harmony. Watching the faces of the church members when KC Wolf walked into the room was priceless. It was obvious this wasn't going to be a typical Sunday morning worship service for them, and when I finished speaking the church members asked if I would dress back up in costume so the they could get pictures taken with KC Wolf.

After lunch the ladies went back to Harmony and presented the second of four women's conferences. While the ladies
were meeting together Pastor Jojo, Danny, Mike and I went to
a tiny church located in an area called Fairview. This area of
the city is considered the slums, as it is surrounded by extreme
poverty. These are the poorest of the poor, but you wouldn't
know it by the way they worshipped. I was convicted as I
watched people who had so little worshipping with such joy. I
was reminded joy does not come from good fortune or worldly possessions. Joy is a mental attitude that comes from appre-
ciating what we have instead of being miserable about what
we don't have. My plan had been to travel to the Philippines
to be a blessing to others, but I found that I was the one being
blessed.

Monday morning we walked to our usual spot for breakfast. The employees at Jollibee's were beginning to recognize
us Americans as some of their regular customers. Afterward
we loaded into the van and drove over to pick up Pastor Ed
and Sister Lucy. They wanted us to see their new church building in San Mateo and introduce us to some of their church
members. It was a beautiful drive through the mountains, and
when we arrived in the village the church members were there
to greet us.

We were served boiled bananas, papaya, avocados, jackfruit
and an assortment of pastries. Some of the ladies from the
church were also involved with the microloan program. They
used their money to purchase produce from the farmers in the
mountains, which they would transport to the city and sell for
a profit. It was evident they were extremely hard workers.
They were also very proud of their new church building. The
church had walls built out of bamboo and a tin roof, which
helped keep the rain out.

As we visited with Pastor Ed and Sister Lucy about their work in San Mateo, they told us many children in the village often got sick. The only drinking water is the water they collect from a nearby stream. Unfortunately, the stream is also used for watering the animals and washing clothes, and the children became ill from drinking the contaminated water.

Ed mentioned they were hoping to raise enough money to drill a new well behind their church so the community could enjoy clean water. When I asked how much it would cost to drill a new well Ed told me they needed approximately $2,000. Without even looking at Cam I immediately knew what she was thinking. The reason I wrote my first book was so we could sell them and use the money to fund projects to help those in need. This was definitely a need we could help meet. The following day we told Pastor Ed and Sister Lucy we would send them $2,000 to drill the well as soon as we got back home. I'm not sure who was more excited–Ed and Lucy because they had enough money to finally build the well–or Cam and me because we knew the well would be a blessing to the entire village of San Mateo.

What I love most about Pastor Ed is that he is a man of action. Two months after our visit to San Mateo we received pictures of children pumping water out of the new well just behind their church, appropriately named the Church of the Living Waters.

Tuesday we dropped the ladies off at Pastor German's church in Minuyan for their third women's conference. Danny, Pastor Ed, Mike and I traveled to three different schools where I presented KC Wolf programs. The first school was a two-year technical college where many of the students spoke English. They asked me to present the program in English without an interpreter, so the students could practice using their English skills. The rest of the day I had to rely on an interpreter. The second program was at an elementary school where I spoke to a group of very excited second grade students. The Philippine teachers seemed to enjoy the KC Wolf visit just as much as the kids.

My final program was definitely the most difficult. I spoke to 350 students at one of the local high schools. Speaking to high school students is always a challenge, and trying to communicate with teenagers who didn't speak my language made it twice as hard. It was a great experience, but by the end of the day, Cam and I were both weary.

The following day we got up early, said goodbye to the Sleep Well hotel, and drove 120 miles north to the province of Pangasinan. We checked into the J'Amore Grand Hotel, and were thrilled to discover that, unlike the Sleep Well, this hotel actually had warm water. It was my first official shower since arriving in the Philippines six days earlier. All week I had been washing my hair in the sink and cleaning my body with a wash cloth. Standing in a shower under warm water felt amazing. Not only did I feel better, but Cam told me I smelled better.

After freshening up we drove to a small church to meet Pastor Romy Vilansana and his wife Dory. Pastor Romy is also a pig farmer. He owns a piggery where he raises pigs and sells them to local restaurants. His piggery was located close to the church. When the wind was blowing you could definitely smell the hogs. Pastor Romy joked it was the smell of money, and the stench didn't seem to bother him at all. Pastor Romy had an interesting way of transporting his hogs into town. He owned a motorcycle with a side car attached. The side car was a large cage made out of steel with a gate on the back. When it was time to take a hog to market, he would open the gate and chase a hog into the cage. Once the hog was in he would shut the gate, start up his motorcycle and away he went. Every time I think about a pastor driving a motorcycle into town with a 200 pound pig riding in the side car it makes me laugh.

What I find even funnier is that every Saturday night Pastor Romy rinses out the pig cage and uses his motorcycle for church transportation on Sunday mornings. For the older church members who have difficulty walking to church, Pastor Romy picks them up and assists them into the side car. He places a board inside the pig cage so his passengers can sit and ride in comfort. Pastor Romy's creativity and problem-solving ability impressed me. It was the first time I've ever seen a motorcycle that served as both a pig and a people taxi.

One of my highlights of the afternoon was the trip to lunch. While everyone else rode into the van with Danny, Pastor Romy drove me to the restaurant on his motorcycle. I can now officially cross *riding to lunch in a pig cage with a pastor in the Philippines* off my bucket list.

After lunch we returned to church, where the ladies presented their final women's conference. Many of the women attending this conference brought along their children. Since childcare wasn't provided, Pastor Romy and Danny gathered the children in a circle outside the church. While they organized the children, I snuck into Pastor Romy's home to change into my KC Wolf costume.

When KC Wolf came bouncing out of the house there was a mixed reaction from the children. Most of the kids laughed, a few screamed, and one little girl stood up and ran straight back into the church to find her mother. It was an extremely hot afternoon, so after 15 minutes of dancing around and taking pictures, I took the costume off and introduced myself. I presented a short program and let each of the children try on the KC Wolf head. It ended up being a very fun day; the children had a great time and the women were thankful KC Wolf and the pastors served as babysitters.

After hugging the children and saying our goodbyes, we loaded into the van. As we drove away from the church the

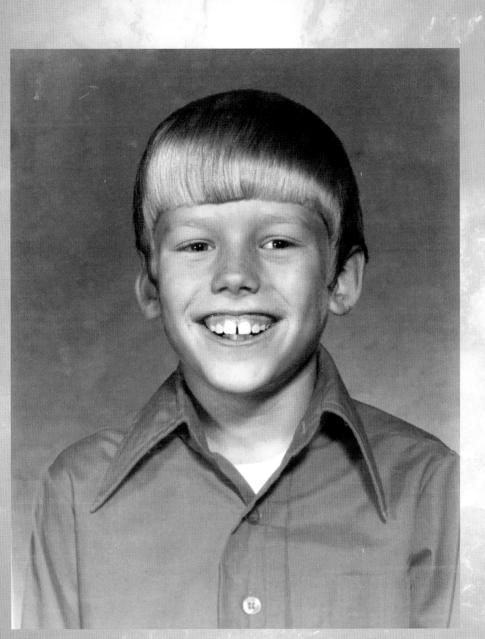

I'm not as young or as good looking as I used to be

Mrs. Laurel Rosenthal has been influencing students for over 50 years

My 102-year-old friends Carmen and Wilma

Delivering 1,544.31 miles of Toilet Paper to Shelter KC

Joe Colazzi has served the homeless for
more than 30 years

Shop with a Cop is a great way to help underprivileged kids at Christmas

The Polar Bear Plunge. One of the only times I've been cold in my costume

Getting a photo with the boys in blue at a Chiefs game

I received the Anchor in the Community Award at the 2017 NFL Mascot Conference

Hanging out in Times Square with my NFL Furternity brothers

Pat the Patriot shortly after losing his battle with a stoplight

My friends and me showing off our dance moves on Waikiki Beach

The mascot calendar photo shoot is always entertaining

The 2018 MLB Mascot conference was held in Kansas City

The Mascot Hall of Fame in Whiting, Indiana

Trying to smile at 124 miles per hour

Preparing to skydive with Mycah and Aaron

Cam and I celebrating our 25th Anniversary

One of my many prom dates at Night to Shine

My brother and I completed the Bike Across Kansas

At the World's Largest Ball of Twine with my dad

Enjoying a coconut with Mike DeBacker and our Honduran friend

Thankfully I had help digging this septice tank

THIS IS CHIEFS KINGDOM

Visiting a senior adult home in Haiti

Yo Quiero Ser orphanage in Honduras,
where my passion for orphans began

KC Wolf celebrating at a festival in Haiti

Ray and Bonnie Van Slyke served as
directors at Grace Mission Orphanage

Grace Mission Orphanage in Limbe, Haiti

The Haitian orphans loved trying on KC Wolf's head

We funded a water well in the Philippine village of San Mateo

The micro-loan program gives women in the Philippines a way to support their families

This motorcycle was used to transport both people and pigs

With the help of an interpreter, I spoke to children in Pangasinan

Enjoying a day at the beach with our Philippine friends

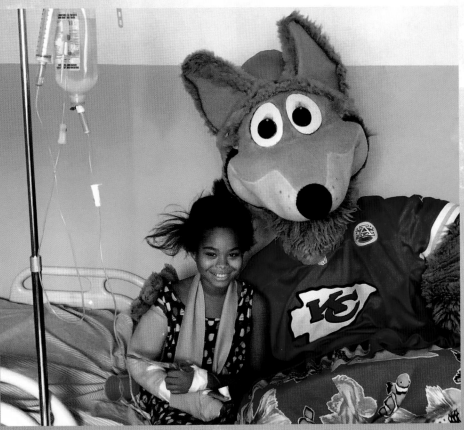

Visiting a hospital patient in San Cristobal

KC Wolf at the DR Mission
Feeding Program

Playing with kids in the
Dominican Republic

KC Wolf attracted lots of attention riding on the back of a motorcycle

My Spanish is terrible. I accidently asked this waiter for a kiss

KC Wolf entertaining children during a DR Missions medical clinic

I had an eventful time at the "Rockathon" in Cuba, Kansas

The Taj Mahal is incredible

This elephant wasn't afraid
of KC Wolf

Riding a camel in
Jaipur, India

It took a while to clean up after celebrating
the Holi Festival with the orphans

KC Wolf visiting a leper colony
in New Delhi, India

Celebrating the Holi Festival

One of the Hope Homes we visited in India

Taking pictures with members of the Assembly of God
Galilee Temple Church in Arusha

Emmrutoto Primary School in Tanzania, Africa

I made many new friends
in Tanzania

These African homes are made
from mud, sticks, grass
and cow dung

I have a passion for helping kids

KC Wolf with children in a Maasai village

Cam, Mycah and Mallory wearing traditional Maasai clothing

Cam and I getting our picture with women from the Maasai tribe

Taking a zebra selfie on our safari

Serving together in Africa is a Meers
family trip we will always remember

After his MVP season we thought about renaming our dog Rusty, Pawtrick Mahomes

Mom and dad are my heroes and role models

Sugar Ray Leonard and me squaring off at a fundraising banquet for the Boys & Girls Club

Miles may be my archrival, but I must admit that horse has style

Cam and I have been married so long we're starting to look alike

I wasn't the only one wearing a grass skirt at the Pro Bowl in Hawaii

KC Wolf wearing pink fur to support Breast Cancer Awareness Month

When your best friend shows up at the party in the same outfit

I'm sexy and I know it…

KC Wolf helps stadium security take care of an unruly fan

KC Wolf and the Chiefs cheerleaders at Abbey Road in London, England

Arrowhead holds the record for being the loudest stadium in the world

Even when it rains, I've still got the best job in the world

After a 30-year career I finally had a chance to go to a Super Bowl.

KC Wolf and Sourdough Sam relaxing on Miami Beach.

Catching some rays on Miami Beach.

Getting a tan before Super Bowl LIV.

Leading the Chiefs onto the field for Super Bowl LIV
is a moment I will never forget.

KC Wolf posing with the trophy
after Super Bowl LIV.

Andy Reid, the coach who helped
get my first Super Bowl ring.

Super Bowl Champions!

My family and me at the Super Bowl parade.

KC Wolf and Captain Fear posing for a photo
before the big game in Tampa.

Super Bowl LV included cardboard cutouts and facemasks.

At the Tour de Donut the Meers boys consumed 31 donuts.

I love living at the lake.

Having Fun in the off-season

Enjoying a boat ride with my family.

The city of Phoenix did a wonderful job hosting Super Bowl LVII.

Patrick Mahomes had a great year. He was voted both NFL MVP and Super Bowl MVP in the same season.

George Toma 'The Sod Father'
has helped prepare the field for every Super Bowl.

Enjoying the Super Bowl festivities with my wife and daughters was one of the highlights of my week.

I tell people that my lucky Sponge Bob Square Pants boxers are the key to the Chiefs success.

My buddy Swoop and I had a good time hanging out together during Super Bowl week.

Winning sure is fun!

There was no shortage of confetti at the Super Bowl rally.

Getting my photo with the Super Bowl trophy alongside
my good friend Shawn Emerson.

My family continues to grow. I'm now the proud father
of five awesome kids.

Your book purchase helps us support orphans around the world— THANK YOU!

children ran behind, smiling and waving goodbye. It made me feel good knowing our efforts had brought encouragement and smiles to both the women and their children. I was reminded again that when you give attention, affection and affirmation to others it's easy to make new friends.

We headed back to our hotel both exhausted and excited, knowing we could take a warm shower and fall asleep in an air-conditioned room. On the way we stopped at a small food shop where Cam and I bought four donuts. The plan was to eat two that night and save the other two for the morning, but the plan quickly changed. We were so hungry, and the donuts were so good, we finished all four off before bed. Nothing tastes better than a not-so-healthy bedtime snack.

Our final day in the Philippines was a play day. We drove to an oceanfront beach just north of Pangasinan province where we spent the afternoon swimming, laughing and of course eating more rice. It was fun spending one last day with several of the pastors we had grown to love. As we traveled back to Manila to catch our plane, I reflected on all the great memories from the week. It was rewarding spending the week with my wife, watching her use her gifts and talents to bless women. I thought about Pastor Ed and Sister Lucy meeting needs in San Mateo. Pastor Danny's smile and infectious personality was spreading love and joy not only to those in his church but also to those who rode in his Jeepney each day. Pastor Jojo was working hard to help educate the young people at his school. Pastor German's leadership was impacting countless lives around the city. Pastor Francis and Pastor Nato were getting ready to move out of their comfort zone and minister to the poor and needy people of Cambodia. And finally, Pastor Romy and Dory, who I will always remember as the pastors with the pig cycle, making an impact in the province of Pangasinan. I admire each of them for the difference they are making in their corner of the world. My friends in the Philippines both inspire and challenge me to look for new ways to be a blessing in the lives of others.

Becoming Mission Minded: Everyone *has* baggage; maybe we should help each other carry it. Who is someone in your life currently struggling with baggage? If you want to live a life of influence, then lend a hand and help them carry it.

11

I Need a Kiss

"I never look at the masses as my responsibility. I look at the individual. I can love only one person at a time. I can feed only one person at a time. Just one, one, one." - Mother Teresa

In the summer of 2018, I packed up my costume and traveled to a country where baseball is the favorite sport. Even though KC Wolf is a football mascot, the children I met in the Dominican Republic (DR) didn't seem to care. They were just excited a costumed character had come to visit them.

I rarely sleep well the night before my trips to other countries because I have a hard time shutting off my brain. Even with my luggage packed and loaded in the car, I still lie awake thinking about all the things I might have forgotten to pack. On this particular trip I finally fell asleep sometime after midnight, and my alarm rang at 2:45 a.m. Like most people, I don't operate well on less than three hours of sleep, but my enthusiasm fueled my energy for the long trip.

I was headed to the DR with pastor Tim Doyle and a group from Restoration Church in St. Joseph, MO. Since they were all driving in from the north and I was the only one who lived south of the airport, I decided to meet them there. My dear friend Rod Handley agreed to pick me up from my house at 3:15 a.m. and drive me. Now Rod is a morning person, but I also know only a true friend agrees to wake up and take me at that ungodly hour of the day. I was thankful, and my wife was beyond thrilled when she learned she wouldn't have to drive me to the airport.

When we arrived, our team immediately started weighing our bags to make sure they were all under the 50-pound weight limit. Each of us had packed one suitcase with personal items and filled an additional suitcase with clothes, toys and other donated items for the orphans and children in the DR. With my KC Wolf costume bag and my personal suitcase, I was limited on how much extra I could pack. I did manage to squeeze in some deflated soccer balls, wiffle balls and an assortment of sports equipment I knew the kids would enjoy.

After checking our bags, we flew to Miami and caught a connecting flight to Santo Domingo. Less than 12 hours after waking up at my home in Kansas City I was standing in the capital city of the Dominican Republic.

Our plan for the week was to work alongside the staff of DR Missions. Rick and Carie Bernard founded DR Missions and began serving in the Dominican Republic in 2003. They operate the Bread of Life feeding program in a very poor section of the city of San Cristobal, and the feeding program provides a nutritious lunch to around 100 children every week day. The Bread of Life program also provides school supplies and basic medical care to the children. Located on the same property as the feeding program, DR Missions also operates the Bread of Life Girls Home. This home houses up to 15 young girls whose parents are either deceased or unable to properly take care of them. The girls are raised in a family-like atmosphere and they assist with the feeding program. The Bread of Life Girls Home and feeding program are located about 15 minutes from the home which houses the DR Mission staff.

When we arrived at the DR Mission, I was thrilled to discover I had a small window air conditioning unit in my bedroom. I knew this would help me sleep much better each night after working in the hot summer sun. We ate dinner together

I NEED A KISS   101

with the staff, followed by an orientation meeting. It was help-ful to know what we could expect throughout the week. It did-n't take long for me to see I would be working alongside a group of people who were passionate about the same thing I am passionate about–ministering to underprivileged children and those less fortunate.

On our first full day in the Dominican we hit the ground running. We traveled to the Bread of Life Girls Home to meet the children and help cook and serve lunch. We arrived early so we would have time to play with the kids. The favorite activity for the neighborhood boys involved in the feeding pro-gram was baseball. They would stand with a bat in their hands and hit balls as long as I kept pitching to them. It was obvious they had played many times because they were excellent hit-ters. Occasionally they would send a ball sailing over the fence that surrounded the girls home, and we would have to wait until someone ran next door to the neighbor's lot to retrieve the ball. Giving up home runs didn't bother me because it gave me an opportunity to take a short break, cool down and rest my arm.

The kids didn't have the nicest baseball equipment, but what they had was put to good use. After playing baseball, we served the kids a meal and then our group headed back to the DR Mission home for lunch. The staff asked if I would put on the KC Wolf costume and do a program for the neighborhood kids at the local park. We decided the best way to get the kids to the park was to put KC Wolf on the back of a motorcycle and drive him through the neighborhood. Apparently, a mas-cot riding on a motorcycle was an unusual sight in the DR because it created quite a stir in the neighborhood.

As I rode on the back of the motorcycle waving, the staff walked behind us inviting the kids to the park. Our strategy worked great because a large group of both kids and adults followed us right to the park. Once everyone was seated, I started taking the costume off. It was fun watching the kids' eyes when I revealed my face. One of the DR Missions staff members interpreted for me as I talked to the crowd about my job. Once again, the highlight was when I dressed up one of the neighborhood boys in the costume. Everyone got a big laugh, and the young man became an instant celebrity among his friends. At the end of the program we took several group photos and eventually sent everyone home with a KC Wolf promotional photo. The program in the park was a big success. For the rest of that week, whenever I walked near the park the kids would all wave and start chanting 'Lobo, Lobo, Lobo' which is the Spanish word for Wolf. Even though the day at the park was extremely hot, it was rewarding knowing my efforts had brought smiles and laughs to so many of the children and adults in the neighborhood.

The next day our service project was at the local hospital. The DR Missions staff was very familiar with this hospital because each week they would go there to pray with the patients. The men would visit the trauma patients, often victims of motorcycle wrecks. The women would visit mothers and babies on the obstetric floor, passing out supplies, new baby clothes, and taking polaroid pictures of the babies for the families to keep.

Our team put together basic hygiene kits, including soap, shampoo and lotion. We placed these items into small zip lock bags so we could give them away to patients and their families. For several years prior, every time I traveled to a hotel I would keep the miniature bar of soap and small bottles of shampoo and lotion. Upon returning home, I would put those items into a small box in my closet. At first my wife thought I was just being a cheapskate and trying to save money on our soap and shampoo expenses. However, what I was really doing was collecting hygiene items to give away on my mission trips.

Anyone who has traveled overseas knows most of the world doesn't live the way we do in the United States. This is especially true in third world countries. I love the USA and am very thankful for my country. However, the more I travel abroad the more I realize how blessed and spoiled we are in America. The little things we often take for granted, like small bottles of shampoo and miniature bars of soap in our hotel rooms, are luxuries in other countries.

The hospital we visited in San Cristobal didn't provide these types of hygiene items. The hospital rooms are constructed of concrete with tiled floors, and each room contains a small bed for the patient. That is it. No pictures on the walls. No couches or recliners for family members. No televisions to watch to help pass the time. In many ways it felt like a very sad and hopeless place for those who were sick and struggling. I'm sure the hospital staff also felt discouraged by their limited resources.

The DR Missions staff felt this would be a great opportunity for KC Wolf to help spread a little joy and laughter. After getting permission from the hospital staff, I dressed up in costume and started entertaining patients and their families. While I walked room to room, the rest of the team visited with the patients and handed out hygiene kits. The families were extremely grateful and kept telling us thank you. Watching the patients' faces light up when KC Wolf walked into their hospital room was all the thanks I needed. I posed for numerous pictures and gave away lots of hugs despite the fact I was sweating profusely through my costume. When we finished up at the hospital, we thanked the staff and headed back to the mission house, where I took a much needed shower.

Sunday morning our team woke up early and drove into town. The DR Missions staff wanted us to experience the sights and sounds of the local market. Hundreds of people gather every Sunday selling produce and clothing items. It is a very festive atmosphere. They had a wide variety of tropical fruits, many of which I had never seen before. We purchased several unusual looking fruits to take back to the mission house so we could taste them at lunch. Not only did I get to experience the sights and sounds of the market, but I also experienced the smells. Several local butchers sell raw meat, and you could always tell when you were getting close to them because the smell was horrific. I'm not sure if the stench attracted customers, but it was definitely attracting the flies.

At home when I smell buttered popcorn at the movie theater it makes me want to buy some. When I smelled raw meat at the meat shops in the DR it made me want to become a vegetarian. At one of the meat shops there was a large pile of chicken feet for sale. The butcher was very friendly. He told me he would give me a good price on them, but I told him there wasn't enough meat on those chicken feet to fill me up. Although he didn't make a sale, he was pleased when I asked if I could take a selfie with him. He and his employee gave me a big smile and thumbs up as I snapped the picture. I thanked them for the picture and they thanked me for stopping by. I wished I had more time to visit with them. In less than five minutes I had made a new friend, a butcher in the DR.

I was very impressed with how kind, warm and friendly the Dominican people were. When we finished our tour of the market our team traveled back to the mission house to grab a bite to eat, and after lunch we drove to the Bread of Life Girls Home for another special celebration.

Rick and Carie Bernard's daughter Brittany, who is married and has four children of her own, had dreamed of hosting a baby shower for all of the pregnant women in the community. When she found out our team from Restoration Church was traveling to the Dominican Republic and serving alongside DR

Missions, she decided it would be a perfect time to have the baby shower. She sent out invitations, organized food, drinks and cake for the party and even had a small baby gift for each woman. Brittany, who works as a nurse, also arranged to have a monitor at the party so the women could listen to their baby's heartbeat.

Many of the women who attended the party were single or did not have a supportive husband to help them during their pregnancy. It was obvious Brittany cared deeply for these women and made sure each one left knowing they were loved. It was funny to watch the men on our team who didn't really know how to act or what to do at a baby shower surrounded by a large group of women. I'm sure we looked like a group of awkward junior high boys standing around at a school dance. When the party ended, the men were excited because we finally knew our responsibilities—eat the leftover cake and pick up the tables and chairs.

Monday was another great day. Once again we were back at the Bread of Life Girls Home helping with the feeding program. We always arrived early so we would have time to play with the kids before lunch. The kids had a special way of making us feel loved. They greeted us with cheers, smiles, hugs and high fives every time we showed up. We can all learn a lot from kids. It made me stop and think about how I make others feel when they meet me.

We spent hours that day playing baseball, soccer and pushing kids on the swing set. After lunch, we played with the kids a little longer before our team headed into Santo Domingo. The DR Missions staff wanted to give us the opportunity to go sightseeing in the capital city, where we had a great time visiting numerous historic sights, taking photos and souvenir shopping.

That evening we went out to dinner at a Chinese restaurant. I thought it was hilarious to be on an island in the Caribbean eating Chinese food. The funniest story of the trip happened while six of us were having dinner at the restaurant. Wes, a member of the DR Missions staff, spoke Spanish so he ordered a wide variety of different Chinese dishes for us to share. He must have really been hungry because he ordered way more food than we could possibly eat. When the meal was finished we still had a tremendous amount of leftovers. We decided we needed about four take-home boxes to pack the remainder of the food.

Wes tried to get one of our team members named Raven to ask the waiter for four take-home boxes, but she was hesitant because she said she didn't feel confident in her Spanish speaking ability. So, I told her I would ask the waiter for the boxes if she would just tell me the words to say. Even though I took three semesters of Spanish in college, about the only words I could still remember were burrito, gracias and buenos dias. I got the waiter's attention, and when he came over to the table Raven told me to say, "Yo neciecito un beso." I assumed this meant, "Can I have four take-home boxes for our leftovers." Instead Raven had tricked me into telling the waiter, "I need a kiss."

As soon as the words came out of my mouth I knew something wasn't quite right because the waiter backed away with a great big smile, and everyone at the table who knew Spanish started busting out laughing. After they informed me what I had said, I also laughed and assured the waiter I didn't want a kiss from him. Growing up, my parents had taught me if I was going to dish out pranks on others then I better learn to take them too. I've dished out my fair share of pranks in my life, but I must admit Raven got me good.

I still laugh when I think about the day I was on a mission trip in the Dominican Republic, eating at a Chinese restaurant and asking my waiter for a kiss while attempting to speak Spanish. We finished our evening in Santo Domingo by going to a French pastry shop and getting dessert. A few hours later I went to bed feeling fat and happy.

We woke up Tuesday morning knowing it would be the last day we would get to spend with the children. Rick and Carie asked me to bring along the KC Wolf costume and put on another program for the kids. I told them I would love to do so as long as a staff member could interpret for me. When we arrived, the children were there to greet us. While they played with the other team members I snuck into the back room and put on my costume.

When I walked out, I was again reminded no matter what country KC Wolf is in, kids and mascots are meant for each other. They go together like peanut butter and jelly. The children were all so pumped to see KC Wolf that the staff had a hard time getting them to sit down and be still for the program. When order was finally restored, I revealed my true identity, showed the kids the costume, and asked for a brave volunteer to try on the costume. Almost every hand shot up. I picked one young man, but because so many other kids asked to wear the costume, I promised I would let each of them try on the KC Wolf head after the program. When I finished, we took several group pictures of KC Wolf with the kids. Then we had them get in a line so they could each put on the head. None of kids seemed to mind that the head was still sweaty from my perspiration.

Watching the excitement and joy on their faces as I placed the KC Wolf head on them was priceless. It made sharing a bedroom at the mission house with a smelly mascot costume each night worth it. While I helped the remaining kids with the KC Wolf head, the other team members served the children lunch.

When lunch was over, we said our goodbyes and headed back to the mission house to prepare for our final service project at the local refugee area. The refugee area is a neighborhood of about 300 families who have all been displaced by natural disasters and flooding in the San Cristobal province. The area where they now live consists of dirty streets and small shanty houses covering approximately two city blocks. It is a very crowded and extremely poor area of the city. DR Missions had formed relationships in the community over the years and regularly helped to provide medical clinics, water filters and solar lights.

Occasionally DR Missions assists with special needs in the community such as building a roof for a new church or passing out mosquito nets to families in need. Our plan this time was to assist with a medical clinic. When we arrived, we carried in multiple loads of medical supplies. It was another hot and humid day, but fortunately the clinic was set up in the shade.

Some of the women on our team worked as nurses in Missouri, so serving at a medical clinic was a perfect fit. I knew how to put on a band-aid, but that was about the extent of my medical knowledge. We decided I should stick with what I did best, which was running around in a costume and entertaining. While the rest of our team helped with the medical clinic, Wes and I walked back to our van so I could change into my costume.

As we walked down the narrow streets of the refugee area, Wes was in charge of crowd control and passing out toothbrushes to the children. Before we left on our trip, DR Missions asked if we could bring toothbrushes along to give away at the medical clinic because the kids were in desperate need of dental care. I talked to my friend Dr. Roger Fender, who is a dentist back in Lee's Summit. He generously donated about 100 toothbrushes and small tubes of toothpaste for us to distribute in the DR. The kids in the refugee area were very excited to see KC Wolf. When we handed them a toothbrush and toothpaste, it was icing on the cake. As I walked the dusty streets, I felt like the Pied Piper with a large group of very happy kids following me. Once again, seeing the smiles and hearing the laughs from the children was more than enough payment for my efforts. When the rest of the team finished treating the last patient, we all climbed back into the van and drove back to the mission house for dinner.

Wednesday was our final full day in the DR, and we spent it hanging out with the DR Missions staff at a resort. It was nice to have a day to unwind before we headed back home. We spent the day laughing, swimming, relaxing and reflecting on our week. I was able to personally say thank you to the staff for their hard work and the impact they are having on so many lives in the DR. It had been a great time, but I was ready to get back home to my wife and kids. I love traveling and serving in other countries, but for me there is no place better than home sweet home.

Thursday afternoon the staff took us to the airport in Santo Domingo, and we said our goodbyes. On the flight back to the United States I reflected on our trip. I thought about all the children and families we met at the Bread of Life Girls Home, the feeding program, the local hospital and in the refugee area. So many people played a role in making the trip a success. Tim Doyle and his team from Restoration Church took care of all the travel logistics and treated me like one of their own. Rick and Carie Bernard and the staff at DR Missions planned out a full itinerary filled with both service projects and fun. Dr. Roger Fender and many other wonderful friends donated items we could give away to children and their families. Finally, my wife, kids and the Kansas City Chiefs organization, who once again supported my crazy dream of taking a mascot costume to foreign countries to spread joy and happiness to the underprivileged. I was thankful for each of them and the significant role they played in helping to impact the lives of others.

Becoming Mission Minded: Who has influenced you and helped make your dreams become reality? Have you told them thank you lately? Are there others you can encourage to fulfill their dreams?

12

A Wolf,
an Elephant and a Camel

*"The difference between involvement and commitment is
like ham and eggs. The chicken is involved
but the pig is committed." - Martina Navratilova*

One thing I've discovered since starting my job as KC Wolf is there are a lot of really nice people in this world, hard working people who are not afraid to get involved. People who are committed to making a positive impact in their communities.

This was never more apparent to me than in 2019. In March I received an email from Lynette Beam, a member of the Cuba, Kansas booster club, asking KC Wolf to make an appearance at their 44th Annual Rockathon. Cuba is a small town in north central Kansas, and they are very proud of their strong Czech heritage.

In 1975, Cuba started an annual fundraising event for their community called the Rockathon. Proceeds from the Rockathon help fund improvement projects for the town not covered in the budget. It's a weeklong celebration event where people from the community secure pledge donations and sit in designated rocking chairs located in the basement of the community building. Virtually all the citizens of Cuba sign up for two hour shifts and literally rock around the clock for a week straight. Each evening the booster club provides entertainment and a meal at the community building. All the proceeds from ticket sales go toward their fundraising efforts.

Lynette asked me to make an appearance and speak on the evening of Friday, March 15. I had never heard of a Rockathon, but it sounded like fun. However, since I was leaving on a trip to India the following morning, I told her that evening wouldn't work for me. She asked if I had any other days available to visit their little town. I checked my calendar and realized I was speaking at the Kickapoo Tribe Boys and Girls Club in Horton, KS on Wednesday, March 13. Cuba was less than two hours west of Horton. Lynette said Wednesday would work great, and I agreed to speak at 7:00 p.m.

When the day arrived, I was excited about getting to experience my first ever Rockathon. After finishing my appearance with the Kickapoo Tribe, I headed west across northern Kansas. Driving into Cuba I passed a sign along the road that read, 'Welcome to Cuba Kansas, Home of the Rockathon.' Since I was running 30 minutes early I decided to turn around and drive back to get a selfie with the sign. I love taking pictures of small town America. My photos help me remember the fun events I get to participate in. Since the sign was located in a field a little off the main road I turned onto a dirt path so I wouldn't have to walk so far. I completely forgot it had rained that morning, and what I initially thought was a dirt path was actually mud. I pulled about 15 yards off the road before realizing I was in deep trouble. When I attempted to put my car in reverse and return to the paved road I realized I wasn't making any progress. When I rolled down my windows, I saw I had made two big muddy ruts. My car tires were just spinning in the mud, going nowhere.

Since there was no way I could get out by myself I called Lynette. I explained to her that I'd gotten stuck out along the highway trying to get a selfie with the Rockathon sign. She laughed and told me she would send her son to pull me out of the mud.

Sure enough, about 10 minutes later a truck showed up with two very nice young men offering to help, but when they backed their truck down the path to pull me out they almost got stuck too. They managed to get their truck back on the pavement but realized it was going to take more than a truck to get me out of my predicament. They made another phone call, and 10 minutes later two more guys showed up with a huge tractor. In the end, it took three phone calls, four nice guys, a truck and a huge tractor to get me to the Rockathon on time. I had a great time entertaining the rockers, and getting stuck in the mud made my trip even more memorable. If you're ever looking for a way to support a great cause by eating great food with great people I encourage you to visit the Rockathon in Cuba.

Three days after I visited Cuba (population 156) I was on my way to the country of India, which has a population of more than 1.3 billion. India is literally on the other side of the world. I was curious exactly how far it was from Cuba, KS. As always, whenever I need a tough question answered I push the button on my mobile phone and ask Siri; she seems to know the answer to everything. Siri informed me New Delhi, India was approximately 7,956 miles from Cuba as the crow flies. I wasn't sure if airplanes and crows fly the same route, but I was excited to learn the airplane I would be traveling on could fly much faster than your average crow.

Although I love getting to visit orphanages around the world, I must admit traveling to them is extremely demanding. My trip to India was no exception. I traveled with a group of seven people led by Steve Morgan from Abundant Life Church in Lee's Summit, MO. We were taking a 10 day trip to India where we would be working with Hopegivers International. Hopegivers works to rescue orphaned, abandoned and at-risk children from the streets. Hopegivers then places the children in one of their Hope Homes, where they are provided with love and care. Children living in the Hope Homes receive 24/7 care including food, shelter, clean water, education and healthcare. Most importantly they are introduced to the love of Jesus and taught they are most precious in God's eyes.

We left Kansas City on Saturday afternoon and flew around three hours to Newark, NJ. We had a five hour layover in Newark before our plane departed for New Delhi, India. The second leg of the trip was significantly more demanding. After closing the doors and giving us the standard airplane safety talk, the stewardess said, "Make yourselves comfortable because our flight time to New Delhi will be 14 hours and 50 minutes." UUUGGGHHH! I felt like I had just received a prison sentence. Mascots are movers and shakers. We hate having to sit down and put a seat belt on for almost 15 hours.

Sitting in an airplane for that long is both mentally and physically challenging. I introduced myself to a nice Indian woman sitting in the seat next to me and learned her name was Pragnya Misra. She lived in India but worked for a company that does consulting around the world. She had been in New York City for two weeks and was returning home. She was very proud of her country and promised me we would have a great time on our visit. It was the last encouragement I heard because about 90 minutes into the flight a baby in the row behind me became upset and started crying. I quickly learned American babies and Indian babies cry in the exact same language…loud.

For the next 13 hours the baby was like clockwork. He would get upset every hour on the hour. Needless to say, when we finally arrived in India I was sleep deprived. Our flight landed around 10:00 p.m. and after picking up our luggage and getting through customs we loaded into a van and headed straight to the hotel. As soon as I checked into my room, my head hit the pillow and I was out like a light.

I woke up the next morning refreshed and excited about experiencing India for the first time. Before leaving on the trip, Steve Morgan had warned us to only drink bottled water. He had previously been on a trip to India and had come down with a disease he referred to as 'Delhi Belly.' I doubt you can find 'Delhi Belly' in any medical journal, but Steve swore it was the worst 24 hours of his entire life. He said one of the symptoms of 'Delhi Belly' is having 'stuff' coming out of both ends, which didn't sound like a lot of fun. I had no desire to experience 'Delhi Belly' so I decided to brush my teeth with bottled water the entire trip.

We first drove to a nearby leper colony in New Delhi, and as we approached the destination I changed into my KC Wolf costume in the back of the van. Changing into a mascot costume in the back of a van filled with people and luggage is no easy task. Traveling with KC Wolf is never convenient, but seeing the smiles on the faces of the lepers who had never before seen a mascot made the hassles of traveling with an extra-large costume bag worth it.

I spent about an hour dressed in costume giving out hugs and taking pictures with people who had spent much of their lives being labeled as untouchables. Many of the lepers gathered at the church, and before we left we sang songs together and prayed for them. I was especially impressed with Pastor Lalmani of the leper colony. He was committed to loving and caring for those who many others tried to avoid. Once again, I felt I had met a modern day hero. Pastor Lalmani isn't rich, athletic or famous. He is just a humble, caring and kind man who does what he can to be a blessing to a group of lepers. He doesn't have much, but what he has he uses to make a difference in the lives of others.

After saying our goodbyes at the leper colony we loaded into the van for a five hour drive to Agra. On this leg of our journey I learned if you're going to ride in a vehicle in India you better have nerves of steel. Words cannot adequately describe the adventure of riding in rush hour traffic in Delhi. It made sitting in Kansas City rush hour traffic seem like a picnic in the park. Delhi traffic is not a place for the faint of heart or for anyone taking high blood pressure medication.

I felt like I was trapped in a van in the middle of 26.5 million people who were all experiencing road rage at the exact same time. It was obvious the India Department of Transportation had wasted their time and money painting lines on the road because nobody pays any attention to the lanes. At one point on our trip I counted nine vehicles lined up side by side on a three-lane road.

Everyone shares the road in India. Cars, trucks, tractors, motorcycles, bicycles, cows, camels, goats, sheep, water buffaloes and even pigs. The driver of our tour van was from Nepal, and I could tell this was not his first rodeo. He was as aggressive as an NFL linebacker. As I observed the chaos I realized the key to being an aggressive driver in India is to use your horn a lot. If nobody pays attention to your horn, don't get discouraged; just keep blowing it.

Thankfully, after a few hours we stopped for lunch at KFC. That's right. After traveling almost 8,000 miles away from the USA we stopped for lunch at Kentucky Fried Chicken. Nothing like some authentic Indian cuisine. After finishing our finger licking good Indian chicken we loaded back in the van and headed to Agra. What was originally scheduled to be a five hour trip ended up being closer to eight hours. Heavy traffic, long lines at KFC and a traveling companion who developed a slight case of 'Delhi Belly' all added time to the trip.

Unfortunately, my fellow team member needed to make several emergency stops at squatty potties along the way in order to take care of business.

The following morning we woke up early and headed out to see one of the Seven Wonders of the World. The Taj Mahal, meaning 'Crown of the Palaces', is an ivory white marble mausoleum, commissioned in 1632 by the Mughal emperor, Shah Jahan, to house the tomb of his favorite wife, Mumtaz Mahal. Our tour guide explained the Taj Mahal took approximately 21 years to build. The construction project employed around 20,000 workers. By the time it was completed the total cost was around 32 million rupees, which in today's US dollars is $827 million. I'm sure I love my wife just as much as Shah Jahan loved his, but after seeing the Taj Mahal it is obvious he had a little more money to spend than me. After touring the Taj Mahal it was also obvious to me why it is such a popular tourist attraction. There is a reason it is one of the Seven Wonders of the World. It is incredible.

I left the Taj Mahal feeling pretty good about myself because in 1999 I also commissioned a building to be constructed for my favorite wife. It was a four bedroom house in Kansas City with indoor bathrooms and a three car garage. Unlike the Taj Mahal my wife's palace was completed in less than a year, and I spent a lot less than $827 million.

After lunch we traveled to the city of Alwar to visit one of the Hope Homes. The mission of Hopegivers International is to provide "Help for today and hope for eternity" for orphans and abandoned children. Cam and I had financially supported Hopegivers for several years, so I was excited to see their work firsthand. They are an organization that shares my passion for loving and supporting orphans. I love that Hopegivers refers to their facilities as Hope Homes and not orphanages. The three interpreters who traveled with us during our time in India all grew up in Hope Homes. J.R, Rajesh and Joshua were all in their early twenties, had graduated from high school, and were working to complete their college studies. It was so encouraging to see three young men who had started out as orphans but are now educated, hardworking and contributing members of society.

When we arrived at the Hope Home in Alwar we were greeted by children who placed a lei of flowers around each of our necks. In the Indian culture a lei or wreath of flowers presented upon arriving or leaving is a symbol of affection. After meeting the children, Andy and Susan Leeper, the directors of the Alwar Hope Home, invited us to have dinner with them. I was excited because one of the menu items was water buffalo. I'm not shy when it comes to trying new foods, and the water buffalo was actually pretty good. During dinner I learned Andy was originally from a small town in South Carolina and Susan had grown up as an orphan in India. God miraculously brought them together through the ministry of Hopegivers, and now they are married and caring for orphans in Alwar.

After dinner I participated in a game of cricket with the kids. Cricket and soccer are the popular sports in India, and the orphans clearly had much more experience playing cricket than me. When the game ended I disappeared into the Hope Home and came back out dressed as KC Wolf. Once again, a mascot appearance was a big hit with the children. We took a lot of pictures and then went into the Hope Home where, with the help of an interpreter, I presented a program for the kids.

We spent the night at a hotel in Alwar and the next day loaded into our van for another long drive to Kota. Our arrival in Kota coincided with a major celebration known as the Holi Festival. Holi is an ancient Hindu festival celebrated predominantly in India and Nepal. It is popularly known as the Indian 'festival of spring', or the 'festival of love'. The Holi Festival reminded me of The Color Run on steroids. It was a free for all festival of colors where people would smear anyone and everyone with colored powder and drench one other with water. Water guns and water filled balloons were used to add to the fun. Everyone on the streets appeared to be fair game. It didn't matter if you were a friend or stranger, rich or poor, man or woman, child or elderly—everyone was covered in bright colors. Our group purchased several bags of the brightly colored powder and took them with us to another Hope Home located near Kota. We spent the afternoon running around and playing Holi with the orphans.

By the time we finished, everyone was in desperate need of a shower. We tried to clean up as much as possible at the Hope Home, and then we headed back into Kota to eat dinner. I went to bed that evening filled with joy knowing I had just experienced a day I would never forget.

Two days later I experienced another day that will forever be etched in my memory. We had spent the night in Jaipur, and we were traveling back to Delhi. It was going to be one of our last full days in India, and we wanted to make the most of it. Along the route we decided to stop and visit the Amer Palace. It is a huge palace located on the top of a high hill. We found out if you purchased a ticket you could ride on an elephant up the hill to tour the palace.

I was so excited; I felt like a little kid on Christmas morning. Since I had never ridden an elephant and I didn't know if I would ever have another opportunity, I decided to put on the KC Wolf costume and try to get a picture. When I stepped up to the platform dressed as KC Wolf I felt like a celebrity because everyone was snapping my picture. The only guy who wasn't thrilled to see me was the man in charge of security. He was afraid I was going to scare the elephants. Just when I thought he was going to ask me to leave, one of the elephant jockeys (I assume that's what an elephant driver is called) motioned for me to climb onto his elephant. I hopped on, and the jockey steered the elephant out into the sunlight so we could get a good picture of KC Wolf.

We snapped several photos, thanked the man for his kindness, and I got down from the elephant so I could take off my costume. After touring the palace our interpreter, Joshua had another surprise for me. As we were leaving town he arranged for KC Wolf to take another ride. This time I was going to be riding a camel. The thought of getting to ride an elephant and a camel on the same day was a dream come true. When we arrived at the camel rides, once again I changed into KC Wolf in the back of our van. When I climbed the platform to sit on his back, the camel stared me down like I was just another rider. I had heard camels like to spit on people, but the camel I rode was very well behaved. The camel man took me on a 20-minute camel ride, and once again our group took a lot of fun pictures. We tipped the camel man with rupees, and I climbed back into the van with a big goofy grin on my face. I felt like a blessed man living a dream. I knew not many mascots get to ride on camels in India. Even fewer get to ride a camel and an elephant on the same day.

Sunday morning I was asked to make another appearance as KC Wolf at one of the local Christian churches. After making the appearance and taking off the costume I was invited to speak. What made this opportunity unique was I spoke barefooted to both Christians and Hindus. It's amazing how something as simple as a KC Wolf costume can bring together people of such diverse backgrounds. We spent the remainder of the day sightseeing around New Delhi. We had a lot of time to kill because our flight wasn't scheduled to depart until 4:30 a.m. On our return trip to the United States we traveled for over 29 hours with layovers in Frankfurt, Germany and Philadelphia.

As I spent time reflecting on my trip to India, I was once again reminded of how many opportunities we had to make a difference in the lives of others. According to UNICEF (The United Nations Children's Emergency Fund), in 2016 there were more than 153 million orphans living in the world. Hopegivers reports more than 31 million orphans live in extreme poverty on the streets of India. Many only experience life in the slums, leper colonies, or on the streets, where drugs and alcohol draw the naïve and scared. These innocent children are starving and alone, and they live daily with the fear of becoming victims of abuse or sex trafficking. All it took for me to make an impact in the life of one orphan was to simply write out a monthly check for $35. I traveled to India because I wanted to see firsthand how Hopegivers was using my donations. I returned from my trip knowing the money was paying big dividends; I could see it in the faces of the orphans at the Hope Homes. I consider it a privilege to team up with organizations like Hopegivers who are committed to making this world a better place for those less fortunate. I'm thankful that during my world travels, I continue to meet many wonderful people who are not only involved but are committed to putting their love for others into action.

Whether I'm rocking in a chair in Cuba, KS or playing a game of cricket with orphans in India, life is most rewarding when I team up with others to make a positive impact in this world.

Becoming Mission Minded: What organization or ministry you could team up with to help change the lives of others who are less fortunate? If you're not familiar with local non-profits, reach out to your church or local Chamber of Commerce.

13

The White Guy
With Hairy Arms

"We all do better when we work together. Our differences do matter, but our common humanity matters more." - Bill Clinton

In June 2019 I had the opportunity to take part in one of the most memorable trips of my life. I went to a school in Tanzania that had just developed a children's feeding program. What made this particular trip so special was my entire family joined me. I had always wanted to travel to Africa, and having my wife and three kids serving alongside me made the trip that much more special.

We traveled with a group from Summit Park Church in our hometown of Lee's Summit. The church had teamed up with an organization called Convoy of Hope, which had been working in Tanzania for several years with children's feeding and women's empowerment programs. The Empowered Girls program was launched in Tanzania and provides secondary school-aged girls with a safe environment to learn about life skills, discuss women's empowerment and health issues and address harmful cultural practices.

Convoy of Hope has been feeding children in Tanzania since 2013. Tanzania's population is around 52 million people, and 44% of them are less than 15 years old. The saddest and most shocking statistic is almost 35% of children under age five suffer from chronic malnutrition. Convoy of Hope works with school and community leaders to build sustainable programs so villages can continue to feed people long after Convoy phases out of a particular location. The goal is for schools to become self-sustaining instead of always relying on handouts. They accomplish this by implementing poultry projects, developing gardens and greenhouses, installing biogas and making school kitchen improvements for efficiency. Our group planned to spend time with the students and help complete the construction of a new kitchen Summit Park Church was funding for Emmrutoto Primary School.

We flew from Kansas City to Detroit, stopped in Amsterdam and then on to Kilimanjaro. Tanzania is exactly 8 hours ahead of Kansas City time, so once again my body clock was all messed up. After 26 hours of travel, we finally landed in Tanzania at 8:15 p.m. on a Friday. We had left Kansas City on Thursday morning. Everyone in our group was extremely tired and very thankful to finally be off the airplane.

I was a little nervous waiting for the KC Wolf costume to arrive. Since KC Wolf travels in an oversized bag, it rarely shows up with the rest of the luggage. Once everyone else had their suitcases, I found the oversize luggage area and claimed my furry friend. After getting through customs we strapped our bags onto the roof of a van and drove about an hour into the town of Arusha. We checked into the Masailand Hotel, ate a late night dinner, and after brushing my teeth for the first time in more than 24 hours, I collapsed into bed.

When I awoke Saturday morning, I was excited to finally get to see Africa in the daylight. I was pleasantly surprised by the cool weather as I grabbed a light jacket. I had always pictured Africa as a dry, hot place, but my first morning in the country it was chilly. As I sat eating breakfast, the hotel waiter pointed out that June is winter in Africa. It was funny seeing the hotel staff walking around in hats and heavy coats although the temperature was only in the 60's. Even during the afternoon, the temperatures were only expected to climb into the mid to upper 70's. I chuckled as I thought about how hard it must be for the people of Tanzania to survive such a brutal winter.

After breakfast we loaded into the van and drove into town. It was fun seeing the excitement on my kids' faces as they experienced African culture for the first time. Our guide for the week was an African named Michael Mlonga. Michael works for Convoy of Hope and helped launch and facilitate the children's feeding programs. Michael is a passionate guy who is very excited about the work being done to impact the lives of young people in his country. He also served as one of our interpreters.

Our other interpreters were two young African ladies named Mayan and Joan. Mayan was a recent graduate from the university. Joan worked as a Nutritionist for Convoy of Hope, making sure students in the feeding program were receiving at least one healthy meal every day. We had a great time getting acquainted with our interpreters, and they were entertained listening to our attempts at speaking Swahili, Tanzania's official language.

One of our first stops was a local school in Arusha. Because it was Saturday there were very few children around the school, but during the week the school averages close to 1,000 students. As we toured the school grounds the school's director showed us the large garden and greenhouses used to support the children's feeding program. Many of the vegetables they grow are used to feed the children, with the remaining sold at the local market. The proceeds from vegetable sales are used to purchase other food supplies for the school.

We also toured a large chicken house located on the school's property where hundreds of eggs are collected each day. The extra eggs are also sold at the local market. Michael is very proud of this school, and it is well on its way to becoming a self-sustaining feeding program.

Our first day in Africa was very relaxing. Convoy of Hope has worked with short-term mission teams for many years, and they know the importance of giving people at least one day to recover from jet lag before launching them into a busy week of service. Karen Carr, our American trip leader, has led overseas trips for many years and is a seasoned traveler.

When we arrived back at the hotel Karen encouraged us not to nap because it would take our bodies longer to adjust to the time change. We decided the best way to stay awake was to go to our rooms, change into our swim suits and meet at the hotel pool. As soon as I jumped into the pool I remembered it was winter in Africa. My plunge into the water took my breath away. It was like taking an ice bath, and after ten minutes of listening to my teeth chatter, my body was totally numb.

Our plan worked perfectly because we were all wide-awake by the time we finished swimming. We spent the rest of the afternoon teaching our African interpreters and drivers how to play a dice game called Zilch. As we sat around a table throwing dice and laughing I was amazed how quickly we began to develop friendships with our African colleagues. In less than 24 hours we had gone from complete strangers to fast friends with a warm and deep connection to one another. Our backgrounds and lifestyles were very different, but we shared a common connection of wanting to help the children of Africa.

Unfortunately, I woke up on Sunday morning at 3:37 a.m. I laid in bed until 5:20 a.m. trying unsuccessfully to fall back asleep. My body clock was definitely not yet adjusted to Africa time. I finally gave up trying to sleep and decided to get up, eat breakfast and start my day. I was scheduled to speak Sunday morning at the Assembly of God Galilee Temple Church in Arusha. With Michael's help as my interpreter I was going to speak during the service and then after church dress up as KC Wolf to take photos with the church members.

The service began with 30 minutes of loud, passionate singing. I was impressed as I listened to them worship. I couldn't understand anything they were singing, but it was obvious they loved the same God as me. When the singing ended the pastor stood up and began to speak. From what I could tell he must have introduced our group to the congregation because everyone looked at us and began to clap.

When Michael stood up and motioned for me, I knew it was my turn to speak. I got up, smiled at the congregation, and said 'Mambo,' which is the Swahili word for hello. Everyone looked surprised and responded by smiling and saying 'Poa,' which translates to 'good' or 'fine.' They were impressed with my Swahili until I told them it was all of their language I knew. Everyone laughed, and the rest of my talk I totally relied on Michael to interpret.

I showed a short highlight video of KC Wolf in action and attempted to explain my job to the church members. I told them how I use my platform as KC Wolf to spread the love of Jesus Christ to people not only in America but around the world. They were excited when I announced I had the costume with me and after church I would put it on so we could take pictures together. When I finished speaking, I went to the pastor's office while he concluded the service. I put on the costume and spent the next 30 minutes taking pictures. I could tell they really enjoyed it because the adults were smiling and laughing just like the kids.

That afternoon our team was scheduled to travel to the small town of Longido in three separate Jeeps. These Jeeps looked like safari vehicles and were specifically designed for traveling on rugged roads. With our luggage stacked on the roofs of the vehicles, we began driving to the Longido

Mountain Village. Before leaving Arusha, we stopped for lunch at a local shopping mall with several restaurant options. I didn't travel to Africa to eat a typical American meal like pizza and a Coke, so I ordered goat leg, french fries and Mango juice. When I finished my meal I couldn't truthfully say it was the best meal I ever had, but it was definitely different.

We were told we wouldn't get very good internet coverage after we left the town of Arusha, so I decided to check my email one last time. I looked at the most current email and the subject line read: AM SO GRAND TO SEE YOUR VIDEOS IN YOU TUBE. The email consisted of a short message, one long run on sentence without punctuation and even a misspelled word, but it made my day. It said: "Hi am peter paschal today we were together at our church TAG Galilee Temple in Arusha actually we enjoyed so much with your talent be blessed."

Peter had gotten my email address off one of the KC Wolf promotional cards we had handed out earlier at the church. He took the time to send me an email thanking me for visiting his church. His thoughtfulness brightened my day, and it reminded me it's often the little things we do, like taking the time to say thank you, which can make a big difference in the lives of others.

We loaded back into the Jeeps and started the two-hour drive to Longido. As we rode, we spotted zebras eating in a field near the road. We asked the driver to stop so we could get out and take some pictures. The only zebras I had ever seen were in zoos back in the United States. In Africa they looked like a herd of striped horses roaming the hillsides. We all agreed Africa's animals were a lot more interesting and exciting than the ones we had back home.

When we arrived in Longido we went out and walked around the village. It was fascinating seeing how different

African culture is compared to what we were accustomed to. Watching the faces of the local residents, it was clear that seeing a group of white skinned people walking around their village was different for them too. There were many people gathered in the streets enjoying the mild weather. As we walked, I acknowledged each person I met with a simple smile and wave. It was a great way to break down communication barriers with people who I didn't share a common language. After touring the village we returned to the hotel for dinner and finished the day by playing another game of Zilch. I went to bed and enjoyed my best night's sleep since arriving in Africa.

The next day we visited Emmrutoto Primary School. The school is a two-and-a-half-hour drive from our hotel at the Longido Mountain Village. The first three minutes of the drive were on a paved road, and then it switched to very rugged dirt roads. Along the way we saw giraffes, ostriches, gazelle, wild donkeys and monkeys.

As we rode, I was stunned by the landscape. In my mind, I had always pictured Africa as a flat, vast desert land covered by dirt and sand. Northern Tanzania was absolutely nothing like what I had pictured in my mind. We drove past beautiful green hills and valleys still lush from the rainy season, and many colorful flowers and plants lined the roads.

When we arrived at the school the children were standing in rows, dressed in purple and singing for us. The best way to describe their singing was loud and proud. They sang their school song and also the Tanzania national anthem. It was fun watching and listening to them perform. They had obviously spent a lot of time preparing for our visit. When they finished singing we met the children with hugs, handshakes and fist bumps. The kids were very excited to meet us because they had never seen white people before. They were fascinated by the color of our skin and our hair. Especially the hair growing on our arms. Many of them had very little hair. In their culture, head shaving is common at many rites of passage, representing a fresh start as one passes from one to another of life's chapters. As a result, I was treated like a rock star simply because I was a white guy with hair on my arms. My daughters both have long hair, which made them really popular with the students.

The majority of the students at the school are members of the Maasai tribe, an ethnic group inhabiting northern, central and southern Kenya and northern Tanzania. They are known for their distinctive customs and dress. We stood out to them because of the color of our skin and our hair, but what we immediately noticed about them was their ears. The piercing and stretching of earlobes is common among the Maasai people. The Maasai women wear various forms of beaded ornaments in both ear lobes and smaller piercings at the top of their ears. They looked very similar to pictures I had seen in *National Geographic* magazines when I was a kid. Now I was getting to visit their village. Being able to carry on a conversation with the Maasai people aided by our translators was really cool.

Michael asked the students to show our group where they walked to get water each day. During the rainy season water is collected from a nearby river, but during the dry season they have to dig a hole deep enough to find water. We walked about 15 minutes, finally arriving at a big hole in the ground approximately 15 feet deep by 10 feet wide. At the bottom of the hole was a small pool of dirty water where the villagers would get water for drinking, bathing and watering their livestock. Convoy of Hope is currently raising money to drill a well on the school grounds so the students and community can have access to fresh, clean water. The plan is to sell the water for a minimal charge and use the money earned to financially support the school. This is another way for Convoy to help the feeding program become self-sustaining.

As we walked back to the school, almost every member of our group was holding hands with multiple children. One of the students holding hands with my son Aaron kept rubbing the hair on his arm and saying "Simba." One of the teachers from the school walking with us laughed and told us "Simba" is the Swahili word for lion. Apparently, the young man walking with Aaron thought he was as hairy as a lion.

When we got back to the school our group saw firsthand how the feeding program works. While the kids washed their hands and got ready for lunch, each of us was given a responsibility. Our jobs included everything from handing out plates and forks to serving the food and collecting the dirty dishes. The whole operation was very well organized, and each student knew exactly what was expected of them. After everyone finished eating and the last plate was collected, we spent the remainder of the afternoon hanging out with the students.

While our group divided up and played a variety of different games with the kids, I slipped into the school office and put on my KC Wolf costume. When I came walking out, the looks on the students' faces were priceless. If they were impressed by a white guy with hair on his arms, I knew a seven-foot-tall mascot covered in fur would really get their attention. I walked into the center of the school yard and began dancing. As the students gathered around me smiling and laughing, I intentionally hugged one of my American friends first. I wanted the African children to realize KC Wolf was friendly, and they didn't need to be afraid. All it took was for one brave student to give me a hug and soon thereafter all the other students mustered up enough courage to hug me as well.

Not only were the children having a great time, but the adults were also fascinated by KC Wolf. I spent the next 30 minutes dancing around the school yard entertaining the Maasai people and getting lots of pictures. When Karen announced it was time for us to leave, I returned to the school office and changed out of costume. I loaded my KC Wolf bag back onto the Jeep and we started the long bumpy drive back to Longido Mountain Village. I was exhausted but felt extremely grateful because my family had just experienced one of the most memorable days of our lives. On the drive back to Longido I couldn't help but smile as I thought about how blessed I was to be able to share this amazing trip with Cam and my kids.

Tuesday morning we woke up and repeated the long drive back to the school. Even though we weren't looking forward to spending another five hours round trip bouncing around in a Jeep, everyone was very excited about getting to spend time again with the students. I rode in the same Jeep as Michael so I could learn more about him and his work with Convoy of Hope.

During the drive, I learned Michael had been married to his wife Edda for 11 years, and they had three children. He has a Master's degree in Business Administration specializing in consulting management and entrepreneurship. Even though he loved business, his true passion in life was working with children. He had spent 13 years with Compassion International ministering to orphans and children before he began working with Convoy of Hope. I could tell Michael loved his job, and he wasn't working solely for the money. Michael told me his motivation comes from seeing children's lives transformed and impacted. Michael is a well-educated man who uses his gifts and talents to have a positive influence on the lives of thousands of children in Tanzania. I respect him greatly and the work he does to impact others.

When we arrived, the students came running into the school yard excited to see us again. After giving out hugs and handshakes we divided up into five groups. Michael organized home visits in the local community so we could get a better understanding of how the Maasai people live. Each group visited a different village near the school. My group walked about 15 minutes before arriving at our village. The village consisted of one man who lived with his five wives and children. Each wife built her own hut made out of mud, grass, sticks and cow manure. In the middle of the village, separating the huts, was an area used as a pen for the goats and cows. The traditional Maasai lifestyle centers around cattle, which is a primary food source. They eat the meat and drink the milk each day. A man's wealth is measured in terms of cattle and children. A herd of 50 cattle is respectable, and the more children the better. A man who has plenty of one but not the other is considered poor.

As we walked through the cow pen, I realized we were visiting a very rich man. I had cow dung on my flip flops, there was a strong smell of cow manure in the air, and kids were running around everywhere I looked. We stopped to visit with one of the wives, and she invited us to see the inside of her hut. She lived with her eight children in a very small hut. The door into the hut was only about five feet tall so all of us had to duck to keep from hitting our heads.

It was very dark in the hut, and Michael turned on his cellphone flashlight so we could see. The inside of the hut contained a small bed for the mother and two cow hides laid out on the dirt floor where all the children slept. In the back of the hut was a tiny area where they stored their corn and corn meal.

When Michael shined the flashlight toward the corn a ground squirrel ran across the floor of the hut. The woman yelled at the squirrel and chased it out through a hole in the back of the hut. She seemed unfazed and calmly told us about her family. I tried to imagine how my wife would have reacted if a ground squirrel went running through our bedroom back home while showing off our house to guests. Something told me Cam's reaction would have been very different. After finishing our visit we went back outside so my son Aaron could go inside the hut. Aaron entered, but he wasn't prepared for how dark it was inside. Before Michael could hand him the flashlight, he smacked his head directly on a wooden pole which supported the inside of the hut. We all got a good laugh when Aaron walked back out of the hut rubbing his forehead.

The funniest part of the entire trip happened on the walk back to the school. One of the students asked Aaron how many children his dad had. Aaron answered, "Three." The student responded, "No, not how many wives does he have, I want to know how many children does he have?" Aaron laughed and said, "My dad only has one wife and three kids." When Aaron told me the story, I had a good laugh. We both agreed while polygamy was acceptable in the Maasai tribe, Cam would not be happy if I had another wife or two. Having multiple wives would be even worse than her discovering a ground squirrel in our bedroom. Although I only have one wife, three kids and don't own any cows, I still consider myself a very rich and blessed man.

When the five groups reconnected back at the school, the women once again helped with the feeding program while the guys painted the school's newly constructed kitchen. The new kitchen was going to be dedicated the following day. They wanted to make sure everything looked great for the ribbon cutting ceremony. The painting project didn't take long, and we spent the remainder of the afternoon playing with the kids.

While Cam taught the girls how to play hopscotch and duck-duck-goose, Aaron held a singalong teaching the students the chorus to the song "Country Roads." Listening to

African children from the Maasai tribe singing a John Denver song was very entertaining. When Aaron finished singing, I demonstrated one of my many hidden talents for the students. I showed them how to make farting noises by placing my hand under my armpit and quickly moving my elbow up and down. Every time I would stop, the kids would giggle and say, "Again, again."

At the end of our day we loaded into the Jeeps and journeyed back to our hotel. Along the route our driver, Peter Huka, pointed out more giraffes and ostriches, and he even spotted some baboons playing in the trees. We were continually amazed at how well he could find animals even when they were attempting to hide in the brush. When we arrived at the hotel, I took a quick shower to make sure I had all the dirt off my body and cow manure off my feet.

When I woke up on Wednesday, June 12, I rolled over in bed and kissed my one and only wife. It was our 26th wedding anniversary, and we were going to celebrate with our three kids in Africa. I told Cam I was thankful I only had to remember one anniversary each year for my one wife instead of five anniversaries for five wives.

We went to breakfast and sat next to Michael. As we were eating, I asked him if he had ever heard of Elvis Presley. I was pleasantly surprised when he said, "Yes, I've heard of him. I like his music very much." I smiled and told him I was also a big Elvis fan. Michael shocked me even more by telling me his favorite music was country music, and his two favorite singers were George Strait and Alan Jackson. It was now officially confirmed; Michael and I were meant to be lifelong friends. Not only did he and I share a passion for working with children, but we also enjoyed the exact same music.

After wrapping up breakfast, we drove back to the school for our final day with the students. About halfway through the trip our driver Peter stopped the Jeep and said he needed to check the tire pressure. He smiled and winked at me as he hopped out of the jeep. The women were concerned we had a flat tire. I assured them Peter was just walking around the back of the Jeep to empty his bladder. Peter had a great sense of humor and liked to speak in code. The day before he had stopped the Jeep and told me he needed to go mark his territory so the lions wouldn't attack the Jeep. Even our drivers were feeling very comfortable around their new American friends.

When we arrived at the school, our interpreter Mayan and one of our drivers named Emmanuel took me back to the village where our group had visited the day before. I wanted to get pictures of KC Wolf standing in front of the mud huts with some of the Maasai women and children. Whenever I travel to foreign countries, I try to take photos to show to students at schools back in the United States. It helps educate them on different cultures and shows them how children from other parts of the world live. Mayan and I decided it would be best if I carried the costume to the village in my bag and then let the villagers watch me get dressed. We didn't want to scare them by having a seven-foot-tall mascot come strolling into their village unannounced. I also didn't want to get chased by a goat or take a chance on getting a spear thrown at me.

Mayan explained to the wives I was going to put on a costume and asked if it would be okay for me to get some pictures taken with them. They all were very interested and excited about the idea. I handed Mayan my cell phone and during the next 20 minutes she took nearly 150 pictures of KC Wolf.

We even took pictures of the children trying on the KC Wolf head, which caused many smiles and much laughter. Once again, I was thankful for my costume. KC Wolf always helps me create positive feelings and easy connections with people who are very different from me. We thanked the women for helping me and showed them some of the photos.

They were fascinated because many of them had never seen a cell phone before. As I packed KC Wolf back into the bag, I looked at the bottom of his shoes. Sure enough, there was cow manure on both shoes. I smiled and pointed at the bottom of the shoes, and the women all started to laugh. I figured this was one of the hazards of visiting the village of a rich man.

When we arrived at the school, the ceremony to dedicate the new kitchen was already underway. This kitchen meant a great deal to the community. Not only were all the students and staff from the school in attendance, but there were government officials, numerous village leaders and hundreds of people from the surrounding area as well. The school yard was packed with Maasai people dressed in their finest outfits. The ceremony included singing, dancing and several speakers. Everyone was very appreciative of all the work Convoy of Hope and Summit Park Church had done to make the new kitchen a reality.

Before the ribbon cutting, our team members stood up and were recognized. Each of us was given a colorful piece of cloth called a Khanga, which was placed around our necks. The American women were given traditional Maasai earrings, while the men were handed colorful beads and necklaces. The community had gone all out to make us feel honored and appreciated. After the ribbon cutting and photos, we joined the government officials and village leaders for a meal in one of the school classrooms. The remainder of the afternoon was spent taking pictures and saying our final goodbyes to the students. As we drove away, I was reminded how quickly relationships develop when people know you care. We helped by providing them a kitchen for their school, and in return they gave us the best gift of all, their friendship.

My Thursday morning got off to a rough start. I woke up early with my stomach acting up. I went to the bathroom three times before 8:30 a.m., which is never a good sign when traveling in a foreign country. I cautiously ate a very light breakfast and took two anti-diarrhea pills. Thankfully, my stomach calmed down, and I felt fine the rest of the day.

We drove to the local bank where we exchanged some of our American dollars for shillings. We then headed to the local Maasai market to buy souvenirs. Back home I hate shopping at the mall, but this market was very different. I had a great time interacting with the shopkeepers and bartering with them over prices. I quickly learned you never pay full price for an item when shopping in Tanzania. Bartering is all part of the game. When we would finally agree on a price, I would ask the shopkeeper to pose for a picture with me along with the item I had just purchased from the shop. They were eager to get their picture taken and were always curious to see themselves in the photo.

After finishing souvenir shopping, we drove two and a half hours to the Farm of Dreams Lodge. This lodge is located in the tourist town of Karatu on the Western south slopes of Ngorongoro Crater, and was by far the nicest of all the hotels we stayed in on our trip. We were all very excited because Convoy of Hope had arranged for us to go on a safari during our final day. The Farm of Dreams Lodge was conveniently located near the Ngorongoro Conservation Area where our safari would begin. Animals in Africa like getting up at the crack of dawn, so our plan was to leave the hotel the following morning at 6:00 a.m. With this being our final night in Africa we decided to stick with our regular routine. We ate dinner, played another game of Zilch with our African friends, and then headed off to bed.

The next morning we left before sunrise. The temperatures were in the 50's, and we all bundled up in our warmest clothes. The Ngorongoro Conservation Area includes mountains, lakes, forests and wide-open African plains. As the sun rose over the Ngorongoro Crater we were amazed at the beauty of God's creation. This crater is one of the 'Seven Natural Wonders of Africa,' and it is easy to see why. When we descended into the crater, our drivers stopped and opened the roofs on our safari Jeeps. They also handed each of us a pair of binoculars so we could get a better look at the animals. The crater floor covered nearly 100 square miles and was mostly grassland. Since the rainy season had just ended, everything still looked very green and lush.

The animals were enjoying the grass buffet, and we saw thousands of them grazing. We spent the morning riding countless miles in the safari Jeeps looking at lions, buffalos, elephants, hippos, ostriches, flamingos, wildebeest, gazelle and zebras. The only animal we wanted to see but never located was a rhinoceros. The Meers family has been on many adventures together, but we all agreed the African safari was one of the best.

After stopping to eat our sack lunches we left the Ngorongoro Conservation Area and headed back to the hotel. We all wanted to freshen up and put on comfortable clothes before driving to the airport. In the hotel bathroom I put my deodorant on extra thick and changed into one of my last clean shirts for the long flight back home.

Komba was one of our drivers I never got to spend much time with because I never rode in his Jeep. During the week I noticed Komba always had a smile on his face, but he was very quiet. When I asked what he had planned for the weekend he told me he and his wife were helping at a home which served blind people in Arusha. His father had started the ministry 30 years earlier, and it was still going strong. He said his father always had a heart for those who were hurting and had taught Komba the importance of caring for those less fortunate. After his father passed away Komba continued to minister to the blind. Obviously, the apple had not fallen far from the tree with Komba.

As we rode to the airport for the long flight home, I thought about our trip and the wonderful people we had met. Most of them looked different, dressed differently, spoke a different language and ate some unusual foods, but deep down I knew we had much in common. We all live together on this big ball called planet earth. We all enjoy laughing. We like to feel valuable, and most importantly we all want to know we are worthy to be loved. We worked together, cared for each other, showed kindness and in one short week a group of complete strangers had become good rafiki's. Rafiki is the Swahili word for friend. We set aside our differences and focused on helping others. Together we provided hope and happiness to a group of Maasai children and their families, and we had a lot of fun in the process. I'm thankful for people like Michael, Komba, Peter, Emmanuel, Joan, Mayan and so many of my other African friends. These people are difference makers living a life of influence and making an impact on the other side of this great big world.

Becoming Mission Minded: Have you ever thought about volunteering your time to go on a mission trip to another country? How about helping out refugees in your local community? You will discover making friends with people of different cultures, whether at home or abroad, is very rewarding.

14

The Best
Groundhog Day Ever!

"Don't put limits on yourself. Not every dream will come true, and not every dream is from God. But when your dreams connect with God's plans, you'll find open doors that you never thought you'd see."
- Max Lucado

I've learned following your dreams is an exhausting, draining effort, but the rewards are well worth it. There have been times in my life when I wondered if certain dreams would ever become reality. Getting to mascot at a Super Bowl was one of those dreams. Several times during my long mascot career, the Chiefs fell just short of reaching the big game. Close, but no cigar. I'm not sure where that saying came from, but it's what my brother Dave and I would say as kids whenever we failed to reach our desired goal. On January 23, 1994, my fourth year in the NFL, the Chiefs lost to the Bills in the AFC Championship game on a cold, miserable afternoon in Buffalo. If we had won the game, I would have made it to the Super Bowl early in my career. Little did I know I would wait another 25 years and perform at more than 250 games before the Chiefs would get that chance again. In 2019, the Chiefs finally made it back to the AFC Championship, but this time the game was played at Arrowhead Stadium. Unfortunately, Tom Brady and the New England Patriots spoiled our party by beating the Chiefs 37-31 in overtime. Once again, we had come one game short of making it to the Super Bowl. At the time I was 52, which isn't exactly a spring chicken, especially in the mascot business. I felt my window of opportunity for performing at a Super Bowl and achieving my dream was slowly starting to close.

The following season the excitement and expectations were very high in Kansas City, and the Chiefs did not disappoint. We finished the regular season with a record of 12-4, clinching the AFC West title for the fourth consecutive time. We received a bye in the first week of the playoffs, then the Chiefs hosted the Houston Texans during the divisional playoff round in week two. The Texans jumped out to a 24-0 lead in the second quarter. KC Wolf was supposed to be the most optimistic fan at the game, but I must admit, even I was feeling that it was going to be another disappointing playoff loss. At one point during the second quarter, a CBS television camera mounted near the Chiefs' locker room, captured KC Wolf banging his head on a door in frustration. This is how every Chiefs fan was feeling at that point. What I didn't realize was the video of me banging my head was broadcast on national television. I like to think my antics somehow inspired the Chiefs because shortly after the video aired, the Chiefs' offense caught fire. We started scoring touchdown after touchdown. We scored 28 points in the second quarter and had the lead heading into halftime. Later in the game the television network showed KC Wolf dancing on the sidelines and slapping high-fives with thrilled Chiefs fans. The Chiefs defeated the Texans 51-31. This victory allowed the Chiefs to host another AFC Championship game at Arrowhead. It was the third time the Chiefs had made it to the AFC Championship during my career, and the third time was a charm. The following Sunday the Chiefs defeated the Tennessee Titans 35-24 to advance to Super Bowl LIV. The victory over the Titans launched two of the busiest and most exciting weeks of my life.

The Chiefs had not played in a Super Bowl for exactly 50 years, and the Kansas City fans were beyond excited. Everywhere you went, people and businesses were showing their support for the team. My phone rang off the hook requesting KC Wolf appearances. Over the next two weeks, in the Kansas City area alone, KC Wolf made a whopping 72 appearances. I was very thankful for my backups, who helped meet the high demand for appearances. I made many appearances in the Kansas City area during the first week, but on Sunday, January 26, I hopped on a plane for the Super Bowl in Miami. The Chiefs sent me and my assistant, Shawn Emerson, along with eight Chiefs cheerleaders and Stephanie Judah, the cheerleader director, to the Super Bowl. We were there to handle the numerous media and promotional appearances.

Shawn and I quickly discovered traveling with eight girls dressed in their matching Chiefs cheerleader sweatsuits created quite a buzz with people at the airport. He and I spent much of our time on the trip serving as photographers for excited Chiefs fans who wanted to get photos with the cheerleaders. I also discovered I wasn't nearly as recognizable or popular as when I was dressed as KC Wolf. Only two people recognized me out of costume, and only one asked to get my picture.

The Southwest airlines employees were very excited when we arrived. They made an exception and allowed us to check in our luggage, even though most of our bags were over the 50-pound limit. My KC Wolf costume bag was definitely over 50 pounds, and apparently the cheerleaders had packed a lot of clothes and hair product for the Super Bowl trip because most of their bags also weighed well over the designated weight limit. The Southwest employees treated us like royalty; when we arrived at our gate, the agent allowed our group to be the first to board onto the plane. As the rest of the travelers loaded onto the plane, most of them made a point to wish us good luck.

When we stepped off the plane in Fort Lauderdale and walked into the airport, we were greeted by Chiefs fans clapping and cheering. For the next 10 minutes we had an impromptu Chiefs pep rally right there at the gate. It was fun to see the excitement on people's faces. After collecting our luggage, we loaded into a van and drove 30 minutes to the Shelborne Hotel on Miami Beach. We checked into our rooms and then met in the hotel lobby to go out for dinner. For the next 2½ hours we ate and talked about the exciting week ahead of us. I couldn't believe I was sitting in Miami dressed in jeans and a t-shirt; twenty-four hours earlier I had been shoveling snow off my driveway back in Kansas City.

Early Monday morning, we met in the hotel lobby and traveled to Robert Renick Education Center. We interacted with students by planting a garden and participating in NFL Play 60 activity stations. When we arrived at the school, I got to see my good friend DC Abramson, aka Sour Dough Sam, the San Francisco 49ers mascot. DC and I had been friends for many years, and I was very excited to spend Super Bowl week with him, hanging out and doing appearances together. Sadly, I learned DC's father had passed away about a week and a half earlier. I had the opportunity to talk with DC and listen to him share memories of his father. Visiting with DC helped me start off Super Bowl week with a proper perspective. Yes, the Super Bowl would be an exciting game with millions and millions of people watching. However, in the big scheme of life, it was just a game, just entertainment. Faith and family are what truly matter. Listening to DC talk about his father I was reminded that relationships are what life is all about. I knew regardless of the final score on Super Bowl Sunday, KC Wolf and Sour Dough Sam were going to walk away good friends.

After the appearance we grabbed lunch and headed back to the hotel. When we arrived, I immediately took the KC Wolf costume up to the hotel room and began blow drying it with a fan I had brought with me. I was glad I had remembered to bring a fan because the heat and humidity in Miami made it very difficult to keep the costume dry. After hanging KC Wolf up, we headed downstairs to a hotel banquet room to practice a dance routine the Chiefs cheerleaders and KC Wolf would be performing later in the evening.

Opening night for Super Bowl activities was held at Marlins Park, where the Florida Marlins play their baseball games. It was a massive facility. There were thousands of fans along with hundreds of media from all over the world there to interview players and cover the Super Bowl. The Chiefs players were introduced and then each player had a booth set up where the media could ask questions. Not surprisingly, Chiefs quarterback, Patrick Mahomes, and head coach, Andy Reid, drew the largest media crowds.

After doing the dance routine with the cheerleaders, I spent the next hour walking around in costume taking pictures and getting interviewed by news reporters from all over the world. I met reporters from Panama, Mexico, England, Denmark, and China, just to name a few. It was fun interacting with them while they tried to do an interview with a mascot who doesn't talk. KC Wolf specializes in answering yes and no interview questions in costume, and eventually I discovered most of the reporters just wanted to get video of KC Wolf dancing. Even though it was extremely hot I had a great time. I used Billy the Marlin's (the Florida Marlins mascot) dressing room, and the best part was he had a washer and dryer. I hand washed my sweaty clothes in the sink and then put them in the dryer. I was sweating profusely through my clothes in the heat, so finding a place to do laundry was a huge blessing.

When I woke up the next morning, I discovered my inbox was once again flooded with emails and phone calls. It was absolutely crazy how many appearance requests were coming in during the week of the Super Bowl. While Shawn and I were busy making appearances in Miami, my backups Jordan, Brady, Moses, and Ky were doing 45 appearances back in the Kansas City area. Realizing the demand for KC Wolf appearances was greater than the supply, I recruited my son. Aaron had been around mascots his entire life, and he'd worn different mascot costumes for me in the past. The Super Bowl madness would be a great opportunity for him to help me out and at the same time earn some extra money for college. Plus, I secretly wanted him to experience firsthand how hard I worked as an NFL mascot.

After a few hours of catching up on my emails and scheduling more appearances, Shawn and I headed to the beach, where we spent several hours relaxing. It was good to get a little down time because I knew the rest of the week would be extremely busy. However, apparently my sunscreen wasn't applied evenly because later I noticed several areas on my body starting to turn as red as KC Wolf's Chiefs jersey! That afternoon we went to the Miami Convention Center where I made an appearance at the Special Olympics Super Bowl with some wonderful kids.

Later, we headed to a Miami Heat basketball game, where KC Wolf and Sourdough Sam performed with Burnie, the Miami Heat's mascot. During a timeout, the announcer introduced us and we squared off at center court. KC Wolf and Sourdough Sam were wearing boxing gloves like we were about to have a prize fight between the Super Bowl contenders. Just as we were getting ready to exchange punches, Burnie came running out and beat us both up. It's an unwritten mascot rule that the home mascot always gets to be the hero in the skits. It was a fun night, and it was good to get to see Vincent Pace, who serves as Burnie. Vincent grew up in Kansas City, and I had done a KC Wolf program at his elementary school when he was young. I reminded Vincent that guys like him made me feel old.

The following morning as we headed out the hotel staff handed us breakfast in a box. Our breakfast consisted of an egg croissant, some mixed fruit, a granola bar, and orange juice. Although I would have preferred a three-egg omelet, I was thankful just to have food in my stomach before starting anther busy day. Our first appearance was at the convention center where we shot a fun piece for the show *Inside Edition*. The reporter was Sailor Brinkley, who I learned was Christie Brinkley's daughter. I had never heard of Sailor, but I remembered her mom, Christie. Every guy at my high school thought she was the best-looking gal on the planet back in the 80's.

After videoing the segment for *Inside Edition*, I took a short break, then headed back out for another appearance with the Chiefs cheerleaders. This one was a Super Bowl live event with hundreds and hundreds of school children participating.

When the event ended, we dropped the cheerleaders off at the hotel. Shawn and I asked our driver, Jose, to take us to Home Depot so we could buy another fan. We had discovered the fan I brought from home wasn't going to be sufficient to keep both of our KC Wolf costumes dry between appearances. Jose was happy to help us out, and after getting the fan we drove back to the hotel. Since we still had a few hours of down time, we decided to get some action photos on the beach of KC Wolf sunbathing. It was fun watching people's reaction to KC Wolf wearing beach attire. We got some great pictures of KC Wolf laying out on the beach, sunbathing, and posing on the lifeguard stand. We also fielded lots of requests to get pictures with the beach goers. The most awkward moment occurred when a lady and her boyfriend walked up and asked to take a picture. KC Wolf usually takes pictures with anyone, but since this lady was missing the top half of her swimsuit, Shawn politely informed her KC Wolf wouldn't be able to pose for the photo. That was a first for me and Shawn both. On the way back from the beach we stopped a guy on a bicycle and asked if we could get pictures of KC Wolf riding his bike. He was very polite and seemed to be entertained, watching as I rode his bike up and down the sidewalk.

Our final appearance of the day was once again at the Super Bowl Live event. The cheerleaders and KC Wolf posed for hundreds of pictures with fans from across the country. It was very hot; the hour felt like it would never end. When the appearance ended, I headed to the mascot locker room and changed. After freshening up I headed to the Super Bowl souvenir shop. Everything was expensive, so I decided to wait until Cam arrived before purchasing souvenirs for my family.

Thursday we had an extremely early start. We met in the hotel lobby at 6:00 a.m. for an appearance on *Good Morning America* and traveled to the Loews Hotel, where they served us breakfast before the live shots began. It was good to get a big breakfast because I had been burning a ton of calories during the week due to the large number of appearances. I did a short 15-second teaser video, along with Sourdough Sam and four of the 49ers cheerleaders. While we waited to film the next segment, DC and I went down to the beach and took photos of KC Wolf and Sourdough Sam sitting next to each other in lounge chairs on the beach. Then we took photos of us walking along the beach together. The photos turned out great, and I used one of them on KC Wolf's Twitter feed. I wrote, "Me and my buddy #SourdoughSam having a stressful week in #Miami #Super Bowl LIV.

After the beach photos, we went back and finished shooting segments for *Good Morning America* then packed up our bags and drove to a local high school. The NFL had paid to install an impressive new football field where the NFL conducted a press conference including the mayor of Miami, the owner of the Miami Dolphins, and Roger Goodell, the commissioner of the NFL.

When the press conference ended, the students went out on the field for a Fuel Up to Play 60 football clinic. The clinic was scheduled to last 90 minutes. I asked Shawn if he would like to dress up as KC Wolf for this appearance. He was thrilled to do it, and I was relieved to get a break after three hectic days. There were several former NFL players helping out. Two of the three were former Chiefs players, Tony Richardson and Donnie Edwards. Tony didn't look like he had aged one day since 2005. Donnie had also kept himself in very good shape. I also met Stephen Jackson, a former running back for the St. Louis Rams. I told him I had grown up in St. Charles, MO which was near the Rams' practice facility. He told me he lived in St. Charles when he played for the Rams, but he was now retired and living in Las Vegas. He was a very nice guy, and all three players were very interactive with the students. After leaving the football clinic, we headed straight to the hotel where we had an hour to get the costumes aired out and smelling better. We doused KC Wolf with some of his favorite FurBreeze cologne and headed to Super Bowl Live at Bayfront Park. I was scheduled to make an appearance for Frito Lay at their Casa de Crunch activation area. Once again, I was performing with Sourdough Sam; our job was to attract people into the Frito Lay exhibit. I wanted to do a good job because Frito Lay was paying big money for the one-hour appearance, and I wanted to give them their money's worth. It's amazing how much companies are willing to pay for appearances during Super Bowl week.

After the appearance I went to the souvenir shop and purchased a miniature football helmet with the Super Bowl LIV logo on it. I then asked Sourdough Sam to autograph it so I could keep it display it with my other football collectibles back at home. After sitting in Miami traffic for 90 minutes, we finally arrived back at the hotel. Shawn and I headed down the street to The Pizza Bar, which was famous for their huge slices of pizza. When we finished eating, we returned to the hotel and saw the Chiefs Flag Warriors standing in the lobby. They had just arrived in Miami, along with the rest of the Chiefs cheerleading squad. We visited with them for a short time then headed to bed; it had been an exhausting day.

The closer we got to the Super Bowl it seemed, the more media requests we received. On Friday, January 31 we all met in the hotel lobby at 5:30 a.m. With the entire cheerleading squad now in town, we divided into three groups. One group went to film *The Today Show*, one group went to *Fox & Friends*, and the group I was assigned to went back to the Loew's hotel to shoot another *Good Morning America* segment. Rob Gronkowski, the former New England Patriots tight end, was also there with us. Even though he had been a major contributor to the Patriots offense the previous year when the Patriots defeated the Chiefs in the AFC Championship game, I tried my best to be nice to him. Rob is actually a very good guy with a great personality. During the segment the cameras filmed Rob running down Miami beach in *Baywatch* fashion with KC Wolf, Sourdough Sam and the cheerleaders in pursuit. When we got to the camera Rob stopped and said, "Welcome to *Good Morning America*." It was a lot of fun, and we got several minutes of airtime. Apparently, many of my friends and family were watching *GMA* because I received numerous text messages saying they had spotted me on TV.

Later Shawn and I, along with the cheerleaders and flag

warriors, headed out to Hard Rock Stadium where the Super Bowl was going to be played. We went to the stadium so we could rehearse our part in the pregame ceremony. As I walked into the stadium for the first time, I got teary eyed. It finally hit me—I was two days away from performing at Super Bowl LIV. I was overcome with how good God had been to me. A 30-year dream was about to become a reality. After locating the dressing room, which I would be sharing with the flag warriors on Super Bowl Sunday, we went to the football field for rehearsal. I learned during the pregame I would be following the flag warriors onto the field. As soon as they ran out, I was supposed to start running as fast as I could because the Chiefs players would be running right behind me. Once again, the thought of running onto the field on Super Bowl Sunday filled me with excitement. THIS WAS GOING TO BE SO COOL. I COULDN'T WAIT FOR SUNDAY TO GET HERE.

I knew the big day was getting close because Cam sent me a text message with a photo of her and our friends Mike and Darla Debacker getting ready to leave Kansas City on the Chiefs' employee charter. The Hunt family, owners of the Kansas City Chiefs, were incredibly generous to their employees. Each employee received two tickets to the Super Bowl, along with airfare and hotel accommodations in Miami. I didn't need my Super Bowl ticket because I was going to be on the field as KC Wolf. This meant Cam and I had a huge problem. We had one extra Super Bowl ticket, along with airfare and hotel for the big game. We talked about giving it to one of our children, but since we have three kids it was very difficult to decide which was our favorite child. Plus, we didn't want to create any family drama. We decided the best thing to do was to give our extra Super Bowl ticket to the DeBacker's. Mike was more than happy to purchase a Super Bowl ticket and an additional airplane ticket to ride on the Chiefs' employee charter. As I looked at the photo Cam had texted me, I could tell their Super Bowl experience was off to a good start. She also texted me a picture of the food options available on their charter flight. The menu included several choices: gorgonzola crusted beef, char-grilled BBQ chicken, cheese ravioli with pomodoro sauce, and salad. Those all sounded much better than the choices I had on my commercial flight down to Miami—pretzels or peanuts.

My only other appearance Friday was the Super Bowl Experience from 3:45-6:00 p.m. Shawn graciously agreed to take the later shift so I could spend a bit of time with Cam and the DeBackers. While waiting in the lobby of the hotel for my ride to the convention center, I received a text cancelling my part. I was super excited because the Chiefs' charter had arrived in Miami, and I could now spend the rest of the day with my wife and friends. Since we were all staying in the same hotel it made it very easy to connect. They decided they wanted to visit the NFL Super Bowl Experience, so we walked from the hotel to the conference center. While Shawn ran around dressed as KC Wolf, I enjoyed the evening dressed in regular clothes. We walked around for several hours looking at the exhibits, browsing through the souvenir shops and buying Super Bowl shirts for our three favorite kids, who were all back at home. We also got our picture taken with the Lombardi Trophy. We finished exploring the NFL Super Bowl Experience and then went out to eat. Since I had to get up at 5:15 a.m. the next morning I decided to sleep in my KC Wolf room. I thought Cam and the DeBackers might want to sleep a little later on their first full day in Miami.

On Saturday, we once again met in the hotel lobby at 6:00 a.m. for yet another appearance on *Good Morning America*, this time with Seattle Seahawks player Cliff Avril. I must admit, appearing on *GMA* three mornings in a row was starting to wear me out.

We went back to the hotel and rested for a couple hours before leaving for the Chiefs pep rally, which was being held at NFL Live at Bayfront Park in Miami. When we arrived, it started to rain intermittently. The pep rally was scheduled from 1:00-2:00 p.m. at the amphitheater. I changed into costume about 15 minutes early so I could get pictures with the Chiefs fans and get them fired up for the rally. I've always loved Chiefs fans because they are loyal, passionate, and fun. When the pep rally began there was music and lots of energy. Mitch Holthus, the voice of the Chiefs, was the emcee, and he always has a way of getting the crowd excited. He is a great guy who is very talented at what he does. The Chiefs Rumble drum line performed first, then the cheerleaders came out and performed a routine. I spent most of my time at the rally dancing, cheering, and throwing out special Chiefs Super Bowl towels. Once again, I was reminded how much people love free stuff. The pep rally was a lot of fun, but the rain caused it to be extremely humid. I was ready to get out of my hot costume and relax. The Super Bowl was now less than 24 hours away and I needed some rest. Shawn agreed to do our final appearance of the day, which was an appearance with the Chiefs cheerleaders at a Zac Brown concert. Since he was covering the concert, I decided to stick around and spend more time at the NFL Live event with Cam and our friends.

The DeBacker's oldest son, Josh, lives in Tampa; he and several other members of the DeBacker family had made the trip to Florida to enjoy the Super Bowl festivities. We met up with all of them and spent the afternoon enjoying the Super Bowl Live activities. After leaving Super Bowl Live we all went to Best Buy. I purchased a GoPro camera, along with a chest mount and a sim card to wear when I ran out for the Super

Bowl pregame introductions. My plan was to run out of the tunnel at the Super Bowl with a GoPro mounted to my head and another one mounted to my chest. I wanted to have video so I could remember and relive the moment for the rest of my life. I also wanted to be able to show it to my family when I returned home. After purchasing the camera equipment, we went to Olive Garden for dinner, because eating pasta is a great way for me to carb load before games.

After dinner, Cam and I Ubered back to the hotel with Mike and Darla. The rest of the DeBacker family went to a different hotel to spend the night. Since they didn't have Super Bowl tickets, they planned to watch the game at Dave and Buster's in Miami. When we arrived back at the hotel, I went to my room to get everything organized for the big day. Shawn was still at the Zac Brown concert, so I had the room to myself. Once again, I reflected on my career and was reminded of just how good God had been to me. I felt blessed so much more than I deserve. As I thought about the game, I was reminded of a Bible verse my college Bible study leader, Larry Glabe, had texted me earlier in the week. It was Psalm 115:1 which says…. "Not to us, O Lord, not to us, but to your name goes all the glory for your unfailing love and faithfulness." I had experienced God's unfailing love and faithfulness. No matter how the Super Bowl turned out I was thankful for all I had experienced over the past week. I had memories, stories, and pictures I would enjoy for a lifetime.

I usually have a hard time getting out of bed each day, but that was not a problem the morning of February 2, 2020. I was very excited and it had nothing to do with the fact it was Groundhog Day. I hopped out of bed and packed all the clothes, for myself and KC Wolf, needed at the Super Bowl. I also included some clothes I was hoping to wear after the game for a Postgame Super Bowl celebration party. After packing I met Cam and the DeBackers in the lobby for breakfast. We decided to sit and eat by the pool, then we went to the beach to take a short walk and take some photos. I was thankful to have Cam with me to celebrate this special day. After the beach pictures we headed back to the hotel so Shawn and I could get to the lobby in time. After 30 years working for the Chiefs, I was not about to be late and miss the bus on Super Bowl Sunday. There was a lot of excitement as the bus pulled away from the hotel and we drove down the highway. I thought about all the blood, sweat and tears I had invested to get to this day. I also thought about all the people in my life who had helped me get to this point in my life. Once again, I realized I was a very blessed man.

When we arrived at the stadium, security was very tight. The KC Wolf bags had to be searched and sniffed by bomb dogs, then we had to go through the usual x-ray scanners to get into the stadium. We walked to our dressing room, laid out the Wolf costume and plugged in our fans. A catered lunch was provided, and then I started stretching out. I knew it was going to be a very long day, and I wanted to make sure I was loose and ready to go.

I made an appearance at the Chiefs Pregame Tailgate Party from 1:30-2:45 p.m. It was great party, with lots of pictures taken with my fellow employees on the trip. Most people don't realize how much hard work goes into an NFL season, so it was very rewarding to celebrate our final game of the season together in Miami. After the Chiefs' tailgate, the security team walked me over to the NFL tailgate party. This was an even bigger party, and people were everywhere. I appeared in the 75 minutes I was there, I saw several Kansas City baseball players who had made the trip to Miami to cheer on the Chiefs. I was able to get a picture taken with Royals players, Alex Gordon and Whit Merrifield. At 4:00 p.m. I went back to the locker room where I changed into dry clothes and attempted to rehydrate. I had already been in costume for 2½ hours in the hot Florida sun, and the game hadn't even started.

Kickoff was scheduled for 6:30 p.m., but the NFL wanted me in costume and ready to go by 5:45. This gave me about 90 minutes to relax. I tried to eat because I knew I would be burning a lot of calories during the game, but because of my nervous excitement I didn't have much of an appetite. It also felt like time suddenly began to stand still. I was excited and ready for kickoff, but it felt like I was trapped in the waiting room at the department of motor vehicles. Each time I looked at the clock it seemed like the hands hadn't moved.

I'm not typically a superstitious guy, but before getting dressed for the game, I made sure I was wearing my lucky boxer shorts. For several years I wore Homer Simson boxers when I performed at Chiefs games. After the 2019 AFC Championship Game loss to the Patriots, I decided to retire Homer. I threw those boxers away and switched to SpongeBob Square Pants. Since my lucky SpongeBob boxers had gotten the Chiefs into the big game, I wasn't about to take a chance and wear anything different on Super Bowl Sunday.

At 5:45 p.m. we gathered in the tunnel leading onto the football field. I received a few last-minute instructions from our NFL game day representative. At Arrowhead Stadium KC Wolf is allowed to roam anywhere he wants inside the stadium; this was not the case at the Super Bowl. He informed me and the cheerleaders we were required to stay on the field in a designated area directly behind the Chiefs sideline. This was fine with me because I knew the San Francisco fans sitting behind the 49ers bench wouldn't have nice things to say. As I looked out over the crowd, I could see the seats were starting to fill up. Cam had told me the section she was going to be sitting in so I waved in that direction, hoping she could see me. I knew it was almost time when Shawn walked over, wished me luck and turned on my GoPro cameras.

After a lengthy introduction video, the stadium announcer came over the loudspeakers at Hard Rock Stadium and welcomed the San Francisco 49ers. As I watched the video board, I could see my buddy, Sourdough Sam, leading his team onto the field. I was excited for my friend because I knew he was looking forward to this experience just as much as me. After the 49ers ran onto the field and made their way to the sideline, the Kansas City Chiefs intro video began to play. As the video played I said a short prayer, but I made sure to keep my eyes open. At this point my eyes were looking directly at the Chiefs flag warriors. I knew as soon as they started to run out onto the field, I was supposed to follow in hot pursuit. The Kansas City Chiefs players were literally going to be on my tail, and I knew they could run a lot faster than me. A 53-year-old man wearing size 23 mascot shoes and 30 pounds of wolf fur isn't exactly known for speed.

When the flag warriors started running, I felt an adrenaline rush and I started running as fast as I could. Apparently, I wasn't running very fast because I noticed several of the players passed me before I even got out of the end zone. By the 10-yard line most of the team had raced past me. Looking back, I think the only person I outran on Super Bowl Sunday was Andy Reid, who wasn't known for his speed either.

After running more than 100 yards, I was breathing heavily as I reached the end zone. I wasn't used to running that far in a mascot costume. I was thankful when I reached the sidelines that it was time to sing the national anthem, which gave me an opportunity to stand still and catch my breath.

After Demi Lovato finished singing the national anthem, the team captains met at midfield for the coin toss. San

Francisco won the toss and deferred, which allowed the Chiefs to receive the opening kickoff. I enjoyed watching all the cell phone flashes going off as the opening kickoff sailed through the air. As I strolled along the sidelines, I realized lots of celebrities attend the Super Bowl. One of the first people I encountered was Alex Rodriguez. Jennifer Lopez was part of the halftime show, and she and Alex were dating at the time. Apparently, you receive a sideline pass if you're in a dating relationship with the halftime entertainment. Since my assistant Shawn also had a sideline pass, I told him his job was to take photos of me with celebrities during the Super Bowl. He managed to get pictures of me with Alex, Howie Long, Tony Gonzalez and Paul Rudd, just to name a few.

I usually take a break during the first half of all Chiefs games, but because I didn't want to miss any of the action during the Super Bowl, I went the entire first half without a break. At halftime I headed to the locker room tired and parched but neither was excited nor depressed, because the score was all tied up at 10-10. The nice thing about the Super Bowl is the halftime show with its big production. As a result, I knew I would get a longer break than normal. I have learned from experience to keep moving during my breaks though. If I sit for too long, my muscles tighten up and it makes getting ready for the second half even more challenging.

Little did I know when I returned for the second half that I would be riding an emotional roller coaster for the rest of the game. At halftime, I made up my mind to get on television in front of the biggest audience of my life. I somehow needed to get behind the goalpost because field goals and extra points are guaranteed television exposure. Even though I had been told to stay on the Chiefs' side of the field, I knew this was a once in a lifetime opportunity and it would be much easier to ask forgiveness than permission. So, I decided to make my move.

During a third quarter TV timeout, I nonchalantly walked from the Chiefs sideline, behind the end zone and positioned myself several yards behind the goalpost. I tried not to get too close to the end zone at first because I thought for sure a security officer would walk over to me and tell me to get back to the sidelines. I spent the next few minutes trying not to draw too much attention to myself. I figured the longer I stood in that spot, the more people would just assume that's where KC Wolf was supposed to stand during the third quarter.

San Francisco began the second half scoring with a field goal. I started to get nervous when Chiefs quarterback Patrick Mahomes threw an interception with 5½ minutes left in the third quarter. Before this turnover, he had never thrown a postseason interception in his career. The 49ers marched the ball down the field and scored a touchdown which gave them a 20-10 lead heading into the final quarter. During the quarter break, I walked back to the sideline and headed toward the opposite end zone as the two teams switched sides. When play resumed, once again I positioned myself under the goalpost as the Chiefs put together a sustained drive early in the fourth quarter. They drove the ball down the field and were inside the 25-yard line. However, Patrick Mahomes threw his second interception of the game when a ball bounced off Tyreek Hill's hands and into the arms of a 49ers defensive back. There were only 12 minutes left on the clock, the Chiefs were losing by 10 points, and the 49ers had possession of the ball. I was beginning to think maybe it just wasn't meant to be. I hadn't given up, but I was getting discouraged as time continued to wind down. I tried to tell myself, even if we lost, I needed to be thankful I had the opportunity to perform at a Super Bowl. With only seven minutes remaining and the Chiefs facing a third and 15 situation, I knew we were running out of opportunities. Suddenly, Patrick Mahomes connected with Tyreek

Hill on a long pass play down to the 49ers 20-yard line. A few plays later Travis Kelce caught a touchdown pass in the end-zone to cut the lead to 20-17. Of course, I made sure to display my dance moves on national television following the extra point. I got really excited when we kicked off and our defense forced to 49ers to punt after only three plays. The Chiefs quickly marched back down the field and scored another touchdown to take the lead. There was only 2:45 left on the clock, and the momentum had shifted entirely to the Chiefs. The 49ers managed to drive the ball to midfield, but once again our defense stepped up and held them on fourth down. Two plays later Chiefs running back Damien Williams raced over 40 yards into the end zone for another Chiefs touchdown. As the extra point sailed through the goalposts, I was dancing with all the energy I had left. The Chiefs had scored three touchdowns in the final seven minutes of the game, and KC Wolf was right there under the goalpost wildly celebrating each one. With only 57 seconds left to play and the Chiefs leading 31-20, I realized we were about to win the Super Bowl. Under the costume I had a combination of sweat and tears streaming down my face.

When the play clock finally expired, I raced out onto the field. Shawn was right beside me with one of the GoPro cameras, trying to capture the moment on video. I paused at the 20-yard line to watch the red and gold confetti falling and listen to the crowd. I was doing my best to take it all in. There was so much confetti falling onto the field that Shawn shot video of KC Wolf making snow angels. I then walked around getting pictures taken with players, coaches, and co-workers. Although I was a sweaty mess, nobody seemed to care. There were lots of hugs and high fives going around. One of the highlights for me was seeing Clark Hunt hold up the Super Bowl trophy. It had been 50 long years since the Chiefs had last won the Super Bowl. I was thrilled and excited for the Hunt family.

After 75 minutes of celebrating, Shawn and us made our way back to the locker room. We each filled our pockets with confetti. We wanted to bring some home so we could share it with friends and family who hadn't been able to make the trip.

When we got to the locker room, we were informed the bus was leaving for the Chiefs postgame Super Bowl party in 30 minutes. As Shawn started packing up my costume, I jumped into the shower. A short time later we were on the bus heading to the postgame celebration at a local hotel. When we arrived, I quickly realized this was going to be the biggest and loudest party of my life. Cam and the DeBackers were going to meet Shawn and I at the party. I tried calling Cam but quickly realized texting was going to be a much better option, as I was having a very hard time hearing. Well known rappers Pitbull and Flo Rida were leading the celebration on the stage. Even though I prefer country music, I could tell most of the Chiefs players were enjoying the rap. After I found where Cam and the DeBackers were sitting, I went to get something to eat. There was no shortage of food to choose from at the party. Football players love to eat, and so do mascots. I was extremely hungry, so I loaded my plate with shrimp, pasta, and a hamburger for starters. I made several return trips to the buffet then moved on to the desserts and ice cream bar. I don't know how many calories I burned during the game, but I know I packed a lot of calories back in at the postgame celebration. We spent the next several hours hanging out at the party and enjoying the festive atmosphere. Around 2:45 a.m. we finally decided it was time to hop on one of the chartered buses heading back to our hotel.

When I got to my room, I unpacked KC Wolf and hung the costume up to dry. I checked my phone and discovered I had received 176 text messages from family, friends, and other mascots from around the country congratulating me on the Chiefs' win. One of the most meaningful texts was from my friend, Sourdough Sam. His text said, "Congrats Brother! No one deserves this more than you. I'm happy our teams got here and I got to share the stage with you. I hope you enjoy the rest of the night and the parade back home. We are truly blessed to do what we do, and I am even more blessed to call you my friend. Love you brother and I will see you soon."

I crawled into bed at 4:00 a.m. exhausted from the day's activities but with an overwhelming sense of God's goodness. I've been blessed with so many wonderful friends and experiences throughout the course of my life. I reflected on His goodness and faithfulness to me during my long career as KC Wolf. During the good seasons and the not so good seasons, God never changed. The Bible says He is the same yesterday, today, and forever (Hebrews 13:8). I'm thankful God always has been good, and God always will be good. God is good all the time. It's who He is. His character doesn't change based upon my circumstances or how I might be feeling. God always has been faithful, and God always will be faithful. Once again, it's who He is. So, whether the Chiefs win the Super Bowl or don't even make the playoffs, I can go to bed each night knowing God loves me and is never going to change. He is the one I can always count on. During my lifetime I've learned God loves His children so much that sometimes He likes to surprise us and allow us to experience things we will never forget. Super Bowl LIV was one of those moments in my life.

Becoming Mission Minded: What dreams has God placed on your heart? How can you use those dreams to have a positive influence in the lives of others? Remember, God uses both our successes and our failures to impact others. With God our past failures never disqualify us from being used in the future.

15

Banana Boy

"We build our lives one choice at a time." - Matthew Kelly

I've never been a rockstar, but I sure felt like one after returning from Super Bowl LIV. Two days after getting back to Kansas City I participated in the biggest parade of my life. Even though the February weather was very cold, more than 700,000 Chiefs fans bundled up and came out to be a part of the biggest party in town. I rode in my warm costume in the back of a pickup truck with Mitch Holthus. Mitch is the Chiefs' play-by-play announcer and is an all-around great guy. He is one of the most enthusiastic Chiefs fans I know. Smiling and waving as we rode along the parade route, we watched confetti fall and listened to fans clapping and yelling. Everyone was dressed in the red and gold Chiefs colors. Fans lined the sidewalks, watched from parking garages and a few even climbed trees to get a better view. The parade ended at Union Station, where we held a Super Bowl pep rally. I was thankful Cam and all three of my kids could join me at the parade. It was a day we will never forget.

Not only was our family celebrating a Chiefs Super Bowl victory, but a few days later we celebrated my son's engagement. Aaron's birthday was on February 9 and he decided this would be the perfect day to propose to his girlfriend, Kyndal Frederick. Everyone in our family adores Kyndal. Aaron planned this proposal for several months and popped the question at the top of the Sheraton Hotel overlooking the city.

Once again, we were in downtown Kansas City, surrounded by family and friends celebrating another one of life's special moments. Life was going great. The enthusiasm for the Chiefs felt like it was at an all-time high. I continued to do lots of appearances over the next five weeks, and then everything came to a grinding halt. COVID. Like all of us, this global pandemic had a huge impact on my daily routine and schedule.

On March 12 the Chiefs informed the staff we would be officing from home for the next two weeks. Little did I know that two weeks would turn into 14 months. Everything changed. From January 1 - March 12, 2020, we made 162 KC Wolf appearances. Over the next 3½ months, through July 1, I made a total of four appearances. Three of those were drive by appearances at nursing homes where I stood in the back of a truck and waved to the residents. The other was a virtual appearance sitting in my basement dressed as KC Wolf in front of my computer. Our lives had changed drastically. On the positive side, I did stay in very good shape because I had plenty of time to ride the stationary bike in my basement. During this time, I was reminded why I loved working for the Chiefs. They had always been very supportive of their employees, and this didn't change during the pandemic.

As the 2021 season approached, we all had lots of questions. Would there be a season? What would it look like? Would fans be in the stands? If there weren't fans, would there be a need for the Chiefs cheerleaders and KC Wolf at games?

It was finally decided the NFL would play the season but with big changes. The Chiefs would hold training camp as usual in St. Joseph, MO, but fans would not be allowed to attend like they had in previous years. Since there weren't going to be fans at training camp, the team wouldn't need KC Wolf to entertain. It was the first training camp I had missed in my 31 years working for the Chiefs. We also found out the

NFL planned to cancel all preseason games. I wasn't too terribly disappointed because preseason games are always the hottest games of the season. I was excited to know the NFL was doing everything it could to make sure the regular season would go on as usual.

The season ended up being the strangest one of my career. The Chiefs limited the number of fans at each game to 22% of capacity. This meant only 16,700 of the stadium's roughly 76,000 seats would be filled. The fans attending sat in pods with their family or friends. Pods were limited to six people and were scattered around the stadium so fans could remain safely socially distanced. Fans wore face masks during the game. It sounded strange because Arrowhead holds the record for the loudest stadium in the NFL, and the facemasks greatly reduced the amount of noise Chiefs fans could create. Tailgating was allowed, but fans could only tailgate with those who also had tickets in their pod. I was very grateful I wasn't the one in charge of gameday logistics. The biggest difference for me was not being allowed on the field. Further, I was supposed to remain socially distanced from the fans while I walked around the stadium. This was extremely challenging because fans are used to giving mascots hugs and high fives. I had two security guys and my assistant Shawn who walked around with me the entire season, making sure fans took socially distanced photos. We even had a custom Covid face mask made for KC Wolf to wear at the games.

Saying the 2020 NFL season was different is a major understatement. Despite all the craziness and changes, the Chiefs had a great season. We finished the regular season with a franchise record 14 wins and qualified for the playoffs for the sixth consecutive year. We defeated the Cleveland Browns and the Buffalo Bills in the playoffs, which gave us an opportunity to play in Super Bowl for the second year in a row. Not only was the regular season different, but Super Bowl LV was also drastically different. The previous year I had spent eight days in Miami at the Super Bowl. This time I would spend only one day on site because of Covid restrictions. We were also limited in the number of people we could bring to the Super Bowl since the NFL reduced the number of paid seats at Raymond James Stadium in Tampa. A few Chiefs cheerleaders and I flew out of Kansas City on the morning of the Super Bowl. Unfortunately, Cam didn't get to join me and my assistant Shawn also didn't get to make the trip.

At the stadium we had to pass through a security screening and get our temperature taken to make sure we weren't running a fever. We were then taken to our dressing area. At Super Bowl LIV, I had a spacious dressing area with multiple lockers, toilets, and showers. In Tampa my changing area was an 8 x 8 foot portable tent set up in a secured area just outside the stadium. Inside the tent was a single table to set my things on and a folding chair to sit on. I was thankful the tent at least had sides so others couldn't watch me dress. The only bathroom was a port-a-potty I shared with the cheerleaders and some other members of the media. Before the game we participated in a pregame tailgate party outside the stadium, where once again we posed for socially distanced pictures with fans. I was excited to see my friend, Captain Fear, the Tampa Bay Buccaneers mascot, who was also at the tailgate party. I was thrilled to get a picture of the two of us together. After the tailgate party I went back to my tent for a short break before heading into the stadium for the start of the game. The other big difference at this Super Bowl was the cheerleaders and mascots were not allowed on the field. I knew I wasn't going to get as much time on television because there was no way I could get behind the goalposts during the game. We were required to remain socially distanced from the players and fans. We spent the entire game cheering from about 30 rows up from the field on the first concourse level on the Chiefs' sideline. In front of us were cardboard cutouts of fans which helped make the stadium look like it was filled. Those cardboard fans weren't nearly as much fun or as loud as the real ones. The cheerleaders were also required to wear masks while they cheered, and they got good at smiling for pictures with their eyes since no one could see their mouths.

By the fourth quarter I realized my lucky SpongeBob Square Pants boxer shorts, which I thought had helped the Chiefs win Super Bowl LIV in Miami, apparently weren't so lucky after all. Even though I was wearing them again for Super Bowl LV, things didn't turn out the way I hoped. The Chiefs scored the first three points of the game but after that went on to lose the game 31-9. After the game I returned to my tent where I tried to wash up using a bottle of water and a t-shirt. It was the closest thing I had to a shower. We loaded back on the bus and headed to the airport. On the way to the airport, I sent a text to Captain Fear congratulating him on their Super Bowl victory. I knew he was feeling the same excitement I had experienced the year before, and I remembered how meaningful Sourdough Sam's text was to me following our Super Bowl victory. After leaving Tampa, it was 70 degrees. When we landed in Kansas City at 2:30 a.m. it had been snowing, and the temperature was 7 degrees. I drove home slowly because of the poor road conditions. A year earlier I had been eating shrimp and having fun with my wife and friends celebrating at the Chiefs' victory party on the night of the Super Bowl. This year I was driving by myself on snowy roads just hoping to eat a bowl of cereal when I arrived home. What a difference a year makes. Despite the disappointment of losing the Super Bowl, I went to bed a few hours before sunrise thankful I had the opportunity to perform at another Super

Bowl. Life was still good. I was sleeping in a warm bed, next to my beautiful wife, with a belly full of bran flakes.

One of the lessons Covid taught me was that our lives can change dramatically, very quickly. Life has its ups and downs. Life can be very unpredictable and challenging. During the pandemic I experienced a range of emotions including frustration, sadness, disappointment, anger, and boredom. One of the blessings of Covid was being forced to slow down, which I'm not always good at doing. It gave me time to reflect on what was truly important. Despite the challenges and frustrations Covid brought, it made me even more aware of God's many blessings I take for granted far too often. I was reminded when hardships and frustrations come our way, we each get to decide how we respond to those challenges. I hope to never go through another pandemic, but I can honestly say I'm thankful for the lessons I learned from living through it.

The following year as Covid began to subside, I could tell people were ready for things to return to more normalcy. Everyone seemed tired of Zoom meetings and virtual gatherings. The number of in-person meetings began to increase. The Chiefs' recent success on the football field resulted in a lot more requests for me to do motivational speaking engagements and KC Wolf appearances. Many of those requests required me to travel out of town. I love getting to meet and talk with so many nice people; doing appearances and speaking at conferences around the country is fun. What I don't enjoy, is traveling to those events. I don't enjoy sitting in airports. I'm tall, so I really don't enjoy sitting in airplanes. I don't enjoy waiting in long lines carrying an oversized mascot costume bag. I don't enjoy eating overpriced airport food. Traveling wears me out, and the older I get, the more exhausted I feel. However, I try not to complain because flying is a lot quicker than driving halfway across the country.

When I go to the airport, I always park in long term parking because it's cheaper. My wife often calls me a cheapskate. I like to think of myself as frugal. It is the reason I never started drinking Starbucks coffee. I am too frugal to drink foofy, expensive coffee. Water is more economical and healthful.

Therefore, I always park in long term parking and ride the shuttle bus to the airport terminal. On this particular trip, I had an early morning flight. When I hopped on the bus it was crowded, but I managed to find a seat near the front directly across from a nice-looking young family. The husband and wife looked to be in their mid-twenties, and they had a cute little boy who looked like he might be a year old. This boy was still dressed in his pajamas, and he looked exhausted.

I sat down with my backpack on, placing my suitcase between my legs so it didn't roll away. As the bus pulled away from the bus stop, I looked over at the boy who was sitting on his dad's lap, facing me. The dad's arm was wrapped around the little boy's waist and the dad was holding a peeled banana in his right hand directly in front of him. The boy was leaning forward, eating away on the banana. I noticed the boy treated the banana like it was a pacifier; he never moved his lips away, he just kept eating. From my perspective, it didn't appear the the boy was swallowing. As he sat there eating, the banana kept getting shorter and his little cheeks kept getting bigger and bigger. I finally smiled at his parents and said, "Your little boy really likes bananas." They both laughed and his mother said, "Bananas are his favorite."

As soon as she had finished telling me about how much her son loved bananas, I saw the little boy's eyes start to close. He pulled his head away from the banana and HAACCH-HOOO! He sneezes. And it wasn't just any sneeze. It was a big projectile sneeze. He blew banana sludge all over me, my luggage and the guy sitting next to me. You should have seen the look on the mother's face. It was a look of sheer terror and panic. As they say in the Southwest Airlines commercials–one of those, *you wanna get away moments.*

As I was sitting there trying to process what had just happened, I glanced at the guy sitting next to me, who was also covered in banana sludge. With a straight face he said, "I sure didn't see that coming," and then busted out laughing. Once he started laughing, I started laughing and at that point, everybody else on the bus realized it was okay to laugh. The only two people who weren't laughing were the little boy's parents. They were too busy apologizing and pulling out diaper wipes so we could clean ourselves up.

I learned two important lessons that day.

1) Never sit directly across from a baby eating a banana.

2) It's not the mess but how you choose to respond that determines your life's story and impact on others.

Yes, the guy sitting next to me could have gotten angry and upset that morning, but all that would have done is make the little boy's parents feel even worse, and it would have made for a really uneasy and awkward bus ride for everyone else. What I appreciated about that man is instead of getting angry, he chose to laugh about it and extend a little grace. Everyone started their day with a good laugh and a great story. When we arrived at the airport terminal, we both smiled and shook hands with the little boy's parents. Then we exited the shuttle bus smelling like we were wearing banana cologne.

Looking back, I can honestly say I'm thankful my life story collided with Banana Boy, his parents, and especially the nice man sitting next to me on the shuttle bus. I am reminded that life is a contact sport. Life can be hard. Life can get very messy at times, but IT'S NOT THE MESS, BUT HOW YOU RESPOND TO THE MESS, THAT IS IMPORTANT. The choice are yours. It's easy to think your life is defined by what happens to you, but the truth is your life, and the impact your life has on those around you, are defined by the choices you make. Often those choices are made in the middle of a mess. It's undeniable, bad things happen all the time. We live in a broken world. We don't always choose right. The people around us don't always choose right. We all get hurt. We all get banana sludge sprayed on us at times. Remember that while you can't always choose what you go through, you can choose how you go through it. You cannot control many of your life circumstances, but you can control how you decide to respond. Like they say, "You can choose whether things make you bitter or whether they make you better."

Pioneer Canadian broadcaster and producer Sydney Banks once said, "Life is like any other contact sport; you're gonna get your knocks. But it's not the knocks that count, it's how you handle them. If you handle them with anger, distrust, jealousy, hate, this in turn is what you're going to get. But if you handle these knocks with love and understanding, they don't mean much. They just dissipate." The same is true for each of us. God allows us to make choices every day, and often times those choices are made right in the middle of a messy situation. The choices you make during those times is what is writing your life's story. Those choices will determine the person you become and the impact your life story has on others.

I often wish my life wasn't so messy. I prefer things being smooth and easy, but honestly this rarely happens in the life of an NFL mascot, it rarely happens for anyone. Pretty much everyone experiences days filled with challenges, disappointments, and frustrations. Sydney Banks was right. Life really is like football; it's a contact sport. The good news is life has something else in common with the game of football. While football is a contact sport, it is also a team sport. Life, too, is a team sport. We need each other. Life is way too challenging and messy to try to do it on our own. We are designed to be together. We were made for community. We are built to need one another, and we are better together.

I was reminded of this on January 30, 2022, when the Chiefs played the Cincinnati Bengals in the AFC Championship Game at Arrowhead Stadium. A Chiefs victory would have sent us to our third Super Bowl. Unfortunately for Chiefs fans, the game didn't turn out the way we hoped it would. Although we were winning 21-3 in the first half, we ended up losing a heartbreaker in overtime. I left that day disappointed, but I also left with a funny story and great life lesson to share with my family. To appreciate the story, I need to share a little background information.

If you ever watch a Chiefs game on television, often you will see KC Wolf under the goalposts when they kick extra points and field goals. The reason is because if my kids weren't at the game, they thought it was cool to see their dad on TV. This fact didn't change even as my kids got older and left our home. They knew they could usually find me under the goalposts after field goals and extra points. It was a great way to get KC Wolf on television.

What usually happened was a couple days before a Chiefs game, one of my kids would call me and say, "Dad, this is what I want you to do under the goalpost this week." Typically, they would suggest some kind of special signal, move or dance they wanted me to perform. It was kind of like our secret handshake or message to let them know DAD LOVES YOU and this move is just for you. So, they would be watching for the move. Well, the week before the Cincinnati Bengals game, the Chiefs played the Buffalo Bills in a divisional playoff game at Arrowhead. It was one of the most exciting games I've ever mascoted in my career. The Chiefs came back with only 13 seconds left on the clock to kick a field goal and send it to overtime. Then they won the coin toss and on the first possession scored a touchdown to win the game.

A few days before the Buffalo Bills game, my youngest daughter, Mallory, called me. Since it was a playoff game, she knew it was going to be played on national television. Mallory had received an athletic scholarship to play volleyball at Louisiana Tech University in Ruston, LA. As a result, she didn't get to attend a lot of Chiefs games in person that season. Mallory called me from her apartment and said, "Dad, this weekend I want you to do the Griddy under the goalpost." I said, "Sure sweetheart, but I have one question. What in the heck is the Griddy?" I had no idea what the Griddy was. She proceeded to tell me the Griddy was the latest dance move all the college kids were doing. She also informed me some of the NFL football players were starting to do the Griddy as part of their touchdown celebration dances.

I decided I would go to the place all old mascots go to learn the latest dance moves; I pulled it up on YouTube. Personally, I thought it was a goofy dance, but since I love my daughter, I spent the week trying to learn the Griddy. On gameday the Chiefs drove down and scored a touchdown. As they lined up for the extra point, I positioned myself right under the goalpost. Right where I needed to be. Everybody else in the stadium was concerned about whether our kicker, Harrison Butker, would make the extra point. I was more concerned with whether I could remember how to do the Griddy.

When the kick soared through the uprights, the crowd went crazy, and I was busy celebrating and showing off my best 55-year-old man Griddy imitation. When I finished dancing, one of the young men who works on the Chiefs grounds crew walked over to me. He tapped me on the shoulder and said, "Wolf, I didn't know you could do the Griddy." Little did he know his comment made my day. I was so proud of myself because he recognized what I was doing.

At halftime I went back into my locker room to take a break. When I looked at my phone, I had a text from Mallory. It read, "DAD, YOU KILLED IT." With renewed confidence I went back out in the second half and showed off my Griddy moves several more times.

With our dramatic win in the books against the Bills, we would now be playing the Cincinnati Bengals in the AFC Championship game. A few days before the game my oldest daughter, Mycah, who lives in St. Charles, MO called me and said, "Dad, I don't care what dance you do this week. I just want you to wear a bunch of different clothes. Every time they kick a field goal or an extra point, I want to see you in different outfit." I had been KC Wolf for 32 years, and I had developed quite a wardrobe, including: Superman, Batman, Spiderman, Captain America, a policeman outfit, tuxedo, Santa Claus, and a wide array of Hawaiian shirts, just to name a few.

The Chiefs came out and scored three touchdowns in the first half. Each time they scored I was sporting a different outfit. I started as Superman and then followed up with a Hawaiian shirt and sunglasses. My final outfit of the half was Spiderman. When the half ended, I walked back to my locker room for my halftime break. As I sat drinking Gatorade and eating a banana, I heard my assistant Shawn start laughing. When I asked him what was so funny, he showed me his phone. A Chiefs fan had posted on social media saying "KC Wolf had more costume changes than a Lady Gaga concert." It was encouraging knowing someone besides my daughter was also noticing my outfits.

During halftime, Shawn and I decided I should start the second half dressed in my Elvis Presley outfit. Several years earlier I had a large white jumpsuit made that resembled the outfit Elvis wore in 1972 at his performance at Madison Square Garden. Big rhinestones decorated the front of the outfit, and a big sequined eagle was displayed across the back. To top it off I had a large gold belt wrapped around my midsection. KC Wolf looked like Elvis during his jelly donut days. The suit was big and gaudy, and the fans loved it. I intentionally left the front unzipped about halfway down so I could show off KC Wolf's chest hair for the ladies. As I walked around the sidelines I stopped and posed for several photos. When I got to the south side of the field, near the Chiefs' bench, I heard an older lady sitting in the front row start screaming. I realized she was a huge Elvis fan, and she was very excited about the thought of getting a picture with KC Wolf dressed as Elvis. I had never seen someone get so excited to have a photo with me. She was waving her hands, yelling at the top of her lungs and doing everything she could to get my attention. As I began walking toward her, suddenly I saw her put her hand up to her mouth. She got a wide-eyed panicked look on her face, and she stood up and started to look around. Then I watched as she leaned over and whispered something to her husband. Her husband immediately jumped to his feet and began to look around.

All the while I'm thinking "this is 'strange.'" I was about to change directions and head for a different section, when I noticed the woman waving me toward her. When I arrived at her seat, she leaned over the rail and whispered, "KC Wolf, I've got a problem. I've got false teeth and when I was yelling and trying to get your attention, they flew out of my mouth and landed down there on the field." I looked down where she was pointing, and sure enough, right there next to my size 23 KC Wolf shoe was a set of teeth. In a quiet voice the little old lady said, "Wolf, can you help me get my teeth?" I nodded my head yes and bent down and picked up her teeth. I tried to be discreet because I didn't want to embarrass her in front of all the other fans. When I handed them back to her, she rinsed them off in her drink and stuck them back in her mouth. Then she asked if she could get a picture. As I began to walk away, she yelled, "Hey Wolf, you're my hero."

Under the costume I couldn't help but laugh. It was the first time in 32 years I had helped someone recover their false teeth at a game. The Chiefs went on to lose to the Bengals, and as I was driving home, reflecting on the game, I thought about the false teeth lady. I learned it doesn't take much to be a hero to someone. You know what I did to become a hero that day? I simply bent down, picked up her teeth and handed them to her. That's it. It was just a simple act of kindness.

Let me ask you a question. Who is someone in your life right now who could use a little help picking up their teeth? Is there a person/co-worker/friend/family member currently in a difficult situation? Who is the person in your life in the middle of a mess and they need a friend? You don't have to do anything big to be a hero, just a small act of kindness to let them know they are not alone.

Life is a TEAM SPORT. This is your opportunity to be a good teammate, a chance for your life story to make a positive impact on someone who is struggling. Look for a chance to be a difference maker in someone's life today.

Becoming Mission Minded: Life is a contact sport – Life is filled with disappointments and challenges. What mess do you currently find yourself in? Remember it's not your mess but how you choose to respond to your mess that determines the impact your life will have on others.

Life is also a team sport—Identify someone in your life who is in the middle of a mess. Who needs help picking up their teeth? Who in your life needs some encouragement? Get involved and be a good teammate. Always remember you can make a big impact on others by doing something small.

16

Tour de Donut

"Reflect upon your present blessings—of which every man has many—not on your past misfortunes, of which all men have some."
- Charles Dickens

I love football, but I must admit by the time I turned 55, I had learned to really enjoy the offseason as well. Offseason gives my mind and my body a chance to recover from the mental and physical demands of performing and representing the Chiefs at innumerable events throughout the NFL season. So, if there was a bright spot to losing to the Cincinnati Bengals in the 2022 AFC Championship game, it was my offseason was suddenly two weeks longer.

Although the Chiefs didn't make it to the 2022 Super Bowl, there was still a lot of excitement about the team and its future. With Patrick Mahomes as our quarterback and Andy Reid as our head coach, there were plenty of reasons for optimism. Although many players would be returning, the Chiefs offense did lose one key contributor. Wide receiver Tyreek Hill, whose nickname was 'the Cheetah' because of how fast he could run, was traded to the Miami Dolphins. Many Chiefs fans were surprised by the trade since Hill had been one of Patrick Mahomes' favorite targets. Some Chiefs fans were even angry Tyreek was leaving for the Dolphins. Personally, I was disappointed he didn't stay with the Chiefs, but I couldn't blame him for leaving Kansas City. I try to put myself in other people's shoes before I get upset with them, and I must admit if someone offered me 30 million dollars a year to work in sunny Miami, I would strongly consider it. Actually, I wouldn't even have to consider it because my wife would make the decision. She would tell me to trade my wolf fur for a fin; for $30 million, I would learn to perform in a marine mammal costume. Unfortunately, I don't think I will ever be in that situation, because mascot salaries likely won't ever increase to this level.

For the first few months of every offseason, I go into maintenance mode with my conditioning. Although it's always tempting to just sit around on the couch and be lazy, I know if I let myself get out of shape from February to July, I will pay the price when the preseason rolls around in August. Riding my stationary bike at least three times a week, along with KC Wolf appearances during the week, keeps me in pretty good shape. The other reason I try to stay in shape is my brother Dave typically signs us up for a bike race during the summer months. After completing the weeklong Bike Across Kansas in the summer of 2017, we decided we should look for shorter bike races. We pedaled 549 miles and both decided it was more than a Meers boy's rear end was ever meant to endure. As a result, we started looking for one-day bike races that were easier on our backsides. In the summer of 2021, we found a race called the Tour de Meers in Meers, OK. Since our last name was Meers we assumed it was a sure sign we were meant to compete. You would think if you shared a name with both the town and the event, and you signed up to compete in the Tour de Meers, they would let you ride for free. Unfortunately, this was not the case, so we paid the same entry fee as everyone else, which included an ugly turquoise blue Tour de Meers t-shirt with a buffalo on the back. Despite my objections, my wife bought each of our children the shirts and just as I suspected, not once have I ever seen my kids wear them.

In the spring of 2022, Dave called me and said he'd found another bike race for us to consider, called the Tour de Donut in Staunton, IL. As soon as I heard the word donut, I told him to sign us up. Other than the light bulb, I've always thought the donut was one of man's greatest inventions. Whoever first decided to take leavened fried dough and add some frosting and sprinkles had to be a genius. It was a clear sign from God we needed to compete in this bike race. I called my son Aaron and asked if he would like to join us. In my family, the apple doesn't fall far from the tree; Aaron is a donut lover just like his father. Aaron decided the Tour de Donut would be a good opportunity to go head-to-head against his dad and his uncle to see who had the strongest legs and stomach. The Tour de Donut was a spoof on the Tour de France, and it was unlike any bike race we had ever competed in previously. This 34-mile race followed lightly traveled roads over rolling terrain. The unusual twist was two refueling stations, one at mile 12 and the other at mile 24, but 'refueling station' was just a healthy way to say donut stop. While donut consumption was not mandatory, the rider would be awarded a five-minute time credit for each donut consumed. Count me in!

When we arrived at Staunton City Park on Saturday, July 9, it was raining. It was definitely not ideal biking weather, but I felt very confident I could eat donuts under any conditions. We checked in at the registration table and proceeded to pick up our 33rd annual Tour de Donut t-shirts. Dave and I both agreed these shirts were much nicer than the ugly Tour de Meers shirts we had received the year before. As I looked around at the other competitors who were gathered at the park, I noticed the bikers appeared to fall into one of three categories. A small percentage had really expensive bikes and looked like serious bikers who were out to win the race. The vast majority of the crowd looked like me, Aaron, and Dave–your average bikers out to get some exercise, have a little fun, and eat some donuts. However, there was another group of men who appeared to be lifelong donut eaters and had to have taken some really deep breaths in order to squeeze into their biking shorts. It was pretty easy to tell by the tightness of the spandex bike shorts who had been training on their bikes and who had been doing their training at the donut shop.

The first 12 miles were relatively uneventful. Aaron, Dave, and I rode together in the rain for about 10 miles and then thankfully the rain stopped. When we arrived at the first donut stop, we parked our bikes and walked to a covered picnic shelter at a small park. The shelter was filled with picnic tables with boxes and boxes of donuts. Unlike most donut shops, which offer a variety of donuts, the Tour de Donut only offered one kind of donut–glazed. When you walked up to the table, you told the volunteer how many donuts you were going to eat. They scanned the bar code on your registration bib for each donut. At the end of the race, you received a five-minute time credit for each donut consumed. Dave was the first to the table, and he grabbed six donuts. I was a little surprised because I was planning to start with four. When Aaron stepped up and asked for six, I knew the family competition had begun. I had been doing a lot of trash-talking leading up to this race, so I wasn't about to let my younger brother and my son out-eat me at the first stop. I stepped up and ordered six myself.

Dave and Aaron decided to use the smash method for eating the donuts. Basically, you stack your six donuts on top of each other and then smash them together into a very thick donut sandwich. It resembles a Big Mac without the two all-beef patties, special sauce, lettuce, cheese, pickles, and onions on a sesame seed bun. Just a big glazed dough sandwich. I chose a different method. I placed a donut around each finger on my left hand, then used my right hand to eat them one at a time. The first two donuts slid down easily, just like they do each Sunday at church. Donuts three and four were a little more challenging but still tasted good. Donuts five and six really weren't enjoyable at all. I washed the six donuts down with a bottle of water, rinsed the glaze off my fingers, and climbed back on my bike. All three of us managed to eat our six donuts in under 10 minutes. It was a new personal best for each of us. I wasn't sure whether to tell my son I was proud of him for that accomplishment or not. The good news was each of us shaved 30 minutes off our time. The bad news was my bike shorts felt like they were squeezing my belly a bit tighter as we pedaled down the road.

Once again Aaron, Dave, and I stayed together while we rode. Since no one was sprinting to get ahead it became obvious this competition was going to be won by the biggest eater. When we pulled into donut stop #2, we parked our bikes and headed straight to the porta-potty. We had been drinking water to stay hydrated, but now we needed to make room in our stomachs for more donuts. After using the restroom Dave stepped up to the donut table. I was hoping he was going to order two at the most. Instead, he asked for three. When Aaron stepped up and grabbed four donuts I cringed. I knew it was time for me to go big or go home. I knew my belly wasn't going to be happy with me, but I also knew if I could keep the donuts down, I would have bragging rights at the next family gathering. It's amazing the stupid things a man will do because of his selfish pride. I stepped up to the table and with as much confidence as I could muster, I said, "Give me six more donuts." The volunteer scanned my badge, and I placed the donuts around my fingers.

For some reason, the first two donuts at stop #2 didn't taste nearly as good as the first two donuts at stop #1, and there was absolutely nothing enjoyable about donuts three and four. I drank some water to help wash them down and get the sugary taste out of my mouth. By the time I finished eating donuts five and six, I sat at a picnic table not wanting to move. More than once in my life I've overeaten at a Golden Corral buffet, but that was on a variety of foods, not just all donuts. The other difference was I've never overeaten at a restaurant wearing biking shorts. Had I been wearing jeans, I could just loosen my belt or unbutton my pants. There was no wiggle room in tight-fitting biker shorts. The worst part was realizing I still had 10 miles to the finish line. The best word to describe eating a dozen glazed donuts in just a little over an hour is painful.

When I saw Aaron and Dave get on their bikes, I knew I had to move. I got on my bike and slowly started to pedal. It was obvious

Aaron and Dave weren't feeling very good either. We didn't set any speed records during the last 10 miles, but we all finished the race, and we each managed to keep our donuts down. Looking along the roadside, not every participant in the Tour de Donut could make that claim. When we got to the finish line we were greeted by numerous family members, including my mom and dad. My aunt Arlene lived in Staunton along with several of my cousins. My cousin Mary came out to take pictures, along with her husband Rich and son Josh. Even though Aaron and Dave both crossed the finish line before me, I ended up beating them because I had a lower adjusted donut time. It was a fun and memorable day. I achieved several career bests: I ate six donuts in less than 10 minutes, and I ate a dozen donuts in less than 75 minutes, all while completing a bike race. The following day at church I skipped the donut table—it was not even a temptation. I did a little research and learned on June 1, 2018, which happened to be National Donut Day, Joey Chestnut set a world record by devouring 257 donuts in just six minutes. I watched the video and noticed Joey was not wearing biker shorts at the time. If Joey ever reads this book, I want him to know his record is safe with me. My days of competitive eating are officially over.

In the weeks following the Tour de Donut, I traded my bike shorts for my swimsuit. Cam and I moved to Lake Winnebago, a nearby Kansas City suburb, in February 2021. We love lake life, especially during the summer. Some of my favorite KC Wolf photos have been taken while playing on the lake. In late July, Chiefs training camp began in St. Joseph, MO. Players returning for training camp was always my signal football season was just around the corner. Our first home game of the season was played September 15 against the Los Angeles Chargers. It was the first Thursday Night Football game broadcast exclusively on Amazon Prime Video and ended up being a very exciting game; the Chiefs managed to pull out a 27-24 victory. This was the first of many victories to come.

The Chiefs finished the regular season 14-3, which matched a franchise record for wins. It was the Chiefs 10th consecutive winning season, which was also a franchise record. The Chiefs clinched the #1 seed in the AFC and went on to defeat the Jacksonville Jaguars in the divisional round. As a result, the Chiefs hosted the AFC Championship Game for the fifth year in a row. I had a hard time believing it was happening again. They say when it rains it pours, and there is no better way to describe my career as KC Wolf. During my first 28 seasons working for the Kansas City Chiefs, we played in the AFC Championship game only one time, back in 1994. The game was played in Buffalo, and we lost. After that game, we experienced a 25-year AFC Championship Game drought, but when the proverbial rain started falling in 2019, it began to pour. For the next five seasons, the Chiefs hosted the AFC Championship Game at Arrowhead Stadium. It's hard to describe the excitement of getting to mascot for those games, on our home turf. On January 29, 2023, the Chiefs defeated the Cincinnati Bengals and earned the chance to play in Super Bowl LVII. It was going to be my third Super Bowl in four years. As I said, when it rains it pours.

Once an AFC Championship game is won, the city goes into a frenzy of Chiefs support in preparation for the Super Bowl. During the following week, most of my time was spent either doing KC Wolf appearances or scheduling appearances. I was bombarded with requests for appearances at schools, churches, nursing homes, banks, grocery stores, and many other companies around Kansas City. I would do appearances during the day, and at night I would return emails and schedule more appearances. The earliest I got to bed that week was midnight. Most nights I was still returning emails around 2:00 a.m.

On Sunday, February 5, my assistant Shawn Emerson and I boarded a plane heading to Phoenix, AZ. We were joined by cheerleading director Stephanie Judah and eight Chiefs cheerleaders. Once again, the Chiefs were sending a group of us a week before the

Super Bowl to handle all the media appearances and other NFL community events. After arriving in Phoenix we immediately went to our hotel. We stayed at the Hilton Phoenix Resort at the Peak. I was excited because this resort had a four-acre waterpark, but I also knew I probably wouldn't get to spend much time there because of a hectic schedule. After settling into our room, Shawn and I headed out to dinner. At Super Bowl LIV in Miami, we had combined to eat 72 inches of sub sandwiches during the week. Our goal at Super Bowl LVII was to break our record. At Subway, we each ordered a footlong sandwich called The Monster. Once finished, we headed back to the hotel.

Our first four days in Phoenix were filled with numerous appearances. Monday's Super Bowl Media Night was held at the Footprint Center, home of the Phoenix Suns. Although I didn't have any speaking interviews, I did receive a lot of requests from reporters asking if they could get video of me showing off my touchdown dance moves. After the event, I managed to get a photo taken with one of the most photographed guys at media night, Patrick Mahomes. One of the best things about Super Bowl week was getting to hang out with Swoop, the Eagles' mascot. Kevin di Girolamo (aka Swoop) and I have been good friends for about 12 years. We usually only see each other once a year, for a day or two at a mascot conference. Kevin is fun both in and out of costume so I was very excited to get to spend the week with him, even if we were cheering for different teams. Shawn and I managed to eat another 24 inches of Subway sandwich on Monday, and then we ate two more footlongs on Tuesday. We had only been in town for three days and had already tied our previous record of 72 inches of Subway sandwiches. A highlight for me on Tuesday was making an appearance with Swoop at the Wheelchair Football Super Bowl. It was inspiring to watch these men play the game of football with so much energy, determination, and passion. It was obvious they were not going to let their handicaps keep them from enjoying the game they loved.

On Wednesday, we had a three-hour appearance at the Super Bowl Experience, which was being held at the Convention Center in downtown Phoenix. Hundreds of students from all over the area came to participate in the NFL Play 60 challenge, which encouraged students to eat healthy and stay active. Guess who sponsored lunch for the students? SUBWAY. After the event there were still lots of extra boxed lunches available for those who had helped. Each box contained several items, including a six-inch sub sandwich; Shawn and I each grabbed two boxes. It was only Wednesday, and we had already obliterated our record by eating 96 inches. Thursday I had an opportunity to participate in an event called Unsung Heroes, a brunch hosted by the NFL to honor those in the area who worked with sexual and domestic abuse victims. NFL commissioner Roger Goodell was in attendance, and he thanked the workers for their efforts and the impact they were making in the lives of others. He and I spent the rest of the morning getting photos taken with this special group.

Friday was our early day. The alarm rang at 3:45 a.m. We had to meet in the hotel lobby at 4:30 to make appearances on national morning television shows. While Shawn traveled with a group to appear on *Good Morning America,* another group of cheerleaders and I rode to State Farm Stadium in Glendale, where the Super Bowl was to be played. We were there to appear on *Fox & Friends.* We arrived before sunrise, so it was still dark and rather chilly. In my costume, the cool morning air felt good. The cheerleaders had a much harder time staying warm in their tights than I did in my fur. We weren't the only ones who got up early. My long-time friend Tony Dungy, former NFL running back Marshall Faulk, and singer Bret Michaels also made appearances on the show. Since I went to high school in the 80s, I was very familiar with Bret Michaels. Many of the younger cheerleaders weren't as familiar with him though, and they confused him with Kid Rock. After we finished we went back to the hotel. When I walked into my room I found Shawn lying in his bed sound asleep. I was also very tired from getting up so early so I decided to take a nap too. When we finally woke up, we headed back to Subway for two more footlongs. Five days into our Phoenix stay we were 10 feet deep into Subway sandwiches.

Later that afternoon I headed back to State Farm Stadium with the cheerleaders, joining a few of the Chiefs flag warriors who had arrived in town. We were doing a walk-through for the Super Bowl pregame. KC Wolf and the flag warriors were scheduled to lead the Chiefs onto the field during pregame introductions, and the NFL wanted to make sure we knew exactly what to do on Super Bowl Sunday. While we were rehearsing, I ran into George Toma, a former Chiefs employee. George is better known as The Sod Father, The God of Sod, and The Sultan of Sod. He earned those nicknames because he had prepared the field for every Super Bowl ever played. At age 94 George decided Super Bowl LVII was going to be his last. He said it was time for the young guys to take over. I couldn't really blame the guy for finally starting to plan for his retirement. I was thrilled to get my picture with him one last time, standing on the field he prepared.

When we finished our rehearsal, we loaded back onto our bus. I was excited to get back because Cam, her friend Kelly Hughes and my daughters Mycah, Mallory, and my daughter-in-law Kyndal were waiting at the hotel. They had all flown in earlier that day. My son-in-law Brendan had to work, and my son Aaron was in med school, so they couldn't make the trip. I was very excited to have all my favorite girls there for the weekend. Saturday I had just one KC Wolf appearance, another NFL Play 60 event held at a local high school. I was excited to have the rest of the day to relax and spend time with my family.

When I got back to the hotel I showered, and the girls and I went to lunch. My cousins Ted and Rhonda Puetz, who live in the Phoenix area, met us for lunch. I hadn't seen them for several years, so it was fun to catch up. My cousin Dale, a huge Chiefs fan, and his wife Casey, was also in town for the Super Bowl, so they joined us. Saturday night we went to the NFL Experience where Shawn was covering our final appearance of the week. It was a rare opportunity to get a picture of my girls and me alongside KC Wolf. Since I'm usually in costume, KC Wolf and I don't get many photos taken together. As I was looking at the picture back in my hotel room, I felt a deep sense of gratitude. I was grateful God had chosen me to be Cam's husband and blessed me with the privilege of being the father to those three girls. All the women in the photo are beautiful, but what I love most about them is that they're all even more beautiful on the inside. Their kindness, character, and love for others are what I admire. Once again, I went to bed reminded I was a very blessed man.

Sunday morning, I woke up excited about performing at yet another Super Bowl. It had been a fun week, but I was glad game day had finally arrived. The bus ride to the stadium was a time of reflection for me. I couldn't help but smile when I thought about the fact I was a 56-year-old man, getting ready to dress up as an active, overweight wolf and perform at the most watched television sporting event of the year. Once again, I was reminded God has a sense of humor.

When we arrived at the stadium, we unloaded our gear and walked to our changing area, where we ate lunch. After lunch, we headed out to make appearances at the pregame tailgate parties. One of the lessons Shawn and I learned in Miami at Super Bowl LIV was doing several hours of tailgate parties before the game and then turning right around and trying to perform at the game was way too much for one guy. Instead of me trying to do both again, Shawn handled the tailgate appearances. We have worked together for so long in costume people can't tell a difference. We look, act, and smell alike dressed as KC Wolf. I went along to the tailgates to take photos. Our first visit was at the official Chiefs tailgate party. It was a very festive atmosphere with lots of food, drinks, and music. After an hour we walked to the NFL tailgate party on the opposite side of the stadium. This tailgate looked like a Christmas party because everyone was dressed in either Chiefs red or Eagles green. Once again there were lots of people, and for the next 45 minutes, KC Wolf posed for hundreds of photos. After a short break backstage, where Shawn was finally able to get a drink and change into a dry shirt, we walked to our final pregame visit at the Chiefs pep rally on the north side of the stadium. This looked more like a Valentine's Day party because everyone was dressed in red. After 30 minutes we headed back to our changing area, where I began to stretch out. Swoop the Eagle had a changing area nearby so I had a chance to visit with Kevin before we suited up. We knew at the end of the game one of us would be disappointed and the other excited, but regardless of the outcome what really mattered was the friendship we shared. We wished each other the best, prayed together, and then went back to our changing rooms to get dressed in feathers and fur.

Forty-five minutes before kickoff we lined up in the tunnel inside the stadium and waited for pregame introductions. They wanted to make sure we were in position early and ready to go. The next 15 minutes felt like an eternity. We were all filled with nervous energy, and time was standing still. When the Chiefs team came out of their locker room and lined up behind us, I knew it was almost showtime. After the Chiefs introduction hype video played, the fog machines went off, and we all raced onto the field. Although I was running as fast as I could, I could see players passing me on both sides. It's hard to outrun professional athletes when you're dressed in a 30-pound costume and wearing size 23 tennis shoes. Listening to the crowd and seeing all the flashing cameras was an adrenaline rush, and I was just trying to take it all in and enjoy the moment. Super Bowl LVII was similar to Super Bowl LIV, as the NFL was very specific about where I could perform. I was allowed on the Chiefs' sideline and behind the end zone painted with the Chiefs logo. The Eagles' sideline and end zone were off-limits. The first half of the game was filled with excitement. After the opening kickoff, the Eagles immediately drove 75 yards down the field and scored a touchdown. The Chiefs responded with a 75-yard drive of their own with a Mahomes to Travis Kelce touchdown pass. The rest of the first half was filled with many exciting plays from both teams, but heading into halftime the Eagles led 24-14. The most concerning thing for Chiefs fans was Patrick Mahomes reaggravating a high ankle sprain he had suffered earlier in the playoffs. I'm not sure who gave the halftime pep talk, but it must have been inspiring. The Chiefs looked like a different team in the second half.

Kansas City received the ball to begin the second half and drove 75 yards in 12 plays. Running back Isiah Pacheco scored on a 1-yard touchdown run to cut the Eagles' lead to three points. The Eagles kicked a field goal on their next possession, but then the Chiefs took over and went on yet another 75-yard, 12-play touchdown drive. A successful extra point gave the Chiefs their first lead of the game at 28-27. Chiefs fans were feeling good and things were about to get even better. The Chiefs forced the Eagles to punt on their next possession. Kadarius Toney caught the punt and proceeded to return it 65 yards to the Eagles' five-yard line. It set a record for the longest punt return in Super Bowl history. A few plays later the Chiefs scored on a four-yard pass play. At that point I was jumping around on the sidelines, feeling very good about the Chiefs' chances. There were just over nine minutes remaining in the game, and I was extremely thirsty. I knew if I was going to take a break, now would be the best time to do so. I wanted to make sure I was hydrated so I didn't have to miss any of the postgame celebrations on the field. I ducked into the tunnel at the far end of the stadium and Shawn grabbed me some water from the Fox Sports coolers.

By the time I finished my break and returned to the field, the Eagles had scored a touchdown and successfully completed a two-point conversion to tie the score at 35-35. I quickly went from con-

fident to concerned. With 5:15 remaining on the clock the Chiefs
began a 12-play, 66-yard drive chewing up most of the remaining
time. With just eight seconds left on the clock, Harrison Butker lined
up for a 27-yard field goal. I desperately wanted to stand under the
goal post as the kick went through the uprights but unfortunately,
he was kicking into the Eagles' end zone where I was not allowed.
Instead, I stood on the five-yard line doing the same thing many
Chiefs fans were doing at that time. PRAYING. I don't know
whether God is a Chiefs fan, but I do know my prayer was
answered. Butker's kick split the uprights, and the Chiefs took the
lead 38-35 with only eight seconds remaining in regulation. The final
play of the game was an incomplete Hail Mary pass.

As soon as the ball hit the ground the confetti cannons started
shooting, and the celebration began. I paused briefly to thank God
for allowing me to be a part of another Super Bowl experience, then
I raced onto the field to get photos taken under a cloud of confetti.
For the next hour, Shawn and I walked around getting photos with
players, coaches, co-workers, and friends. Cam's seat was on the
upper deck, but she managed to make her way down to the front
row we could get a picture taken together. After such a long and
demanding season I was thankful to get to celebrate with my wife
who'd had to put up with my crazy schedule. After my photo with
Cam, there was still one picture I really wanted. KC Wolf holding the
Super Bowl trophy. Shawn and I walked up onto the stage, and he
snapped several photos of me holding the Vince Lombardi Trophy.
After filling our pockets with confetti we walked off the field and
headed to our changing area.

Our next stop was the postgame party at the players' hotel. I
quickly took off my KC Wolf costume and packed him in his travel
bag. Since there wasn't a shower in my changing area, I put on my
clothes and gave myself a cologne bath to cover up the smell. I knew
after a Chiefs Super Bowl victory the crowd doesn't really care how
you look or smell at the party. Winning put everyone in a good

mood. What I was most excited about was even though my daughters weren't able to attend the Super Bowl, I did manage to get them tickets for the postgame party. They were very excited to see the Chiefs players and they were also thrilled to find out The Chainsmokers, DJ Khaled, and Jason Derulo would all be performing at the party. Personally, I was more excited about the postgame party food. The party was just what I expected. Lots of food, drinks and very loud music. It was a great way to finish off a very long season. At 2:00 a.m. we hopped on the last shuttle bus and headed back to our hotel where I showered and collapsed into bed. The following day we returned home, and two days later I was blessed by participating in another Super Bowl parade through the streets of Kansas City. It had been 17 busy, exciting, crazy, fun, hectic, exhausting, awesome days since the Chiefs had won the AFC Championship game. Seventeen days filled with so many incredible experiences and memories I will never forget.

Winning Super Bowl LVII was great. Winning is always more fun than losing. However, as I've gotten older, win or lose, I've learned the most important thing for me is to appreciate and be thankful for the experience. My life has been filled with so many experiences–some good and some not so pleasant which have combined to make me the man I am today, shaping my life story. As a mascot I've learned despite my best efforts, I really don't have much control over the outcome of a football game. The same is true in my life. Despite my best efforts, I don't always have control over what happens. I like to think I'm in control. I like when everything goes according to my plan and my wishes. However, I've learned it's better for my mental and physical health when I accept the fact I'm not in control. Things don't always turn out the way I want. Sometimes my prayers don't get answered the way I want. Sometimes life isn't fair. I can't always control what happens, but I can control my response. I'm still learning the best way to live life is to trust in a God who loves me even when I don't see or understand His ways. This old mascot has learned living with a heart filled with thankfulness and gratitude is the best way to respond to life's challenges.

Becoming Mission Minded: How can you use your life experiences–the good, the bad, and the ugly, to encourage someone else who is currently going through a struggle? Your life is your story. Write well. Edit often. Write a life story for yourself that is a book worth reading.

17

The Real Me

"He who lays up treasures on earth spends his life backing away from his treasures. To him, death is loss. He who lays up treasures in heaven looks forward to eternity; he's moving daily toward his treasures. To him, death is gain." - Randy Alcorn

Like most people I have many titles in my life. Depending on who you talk to I'm known as a husband, father, son, brother, brother in law, nephew, uncle, friend, neighbor or co-worker. Although those titles tell you the relationship I have with others, it doesn't tell you who I am.

To thousands of people in the Kansas City area I'm known as KC Wolf, the Chiefs mascot. Once again, the title KC Wolf doesn't tell you who I really am, it only tells what I do. Throughout my career I've always enjoyed getting to meet Chiefs fans, both in and out of costume. I've worked with the Chiefs for more than 30 years and have done so many public appearances that occasionally people recognize me even when I'm not in costume.

I'm always amused when I'm out in public and can tell someone is watching me from a distance. After awhile they usually get up the nerve to come over and say, "Excuse me for asking, but are you KC Wolf?" I usually respond by smiling and saying, "I'm really, really good friends with him. We smell alike most days." Yes, KC Wolf is my job title, it is what I do, but KC Wolf is not who I am. KC Wolf is not my true identity. I once heard the two most important times in a man's life are when he finally discovers WHO he is (his true IDENTITY) and

WHY he is (his PURPOSE). I must admit, like most people it took me a while to discover both.

Thinking back on my childhood, I realize my identity was often wrapped up in what I did. My identity primarily centered around my activities, so it constantly changed based upon the season of the year. Since I loved playing sports, I often found my identity on the field or on the court. In the summer I was Danny Meers the baseball player, but by the fall my identity changed to Danny Meers the basketball player.

As I grew older and participated in more activities not only did my identity keep changing, but so did my name. In elementary school my friends called me Danny. In junior high they started calling me Dan. Even my own family members changed my name. When I was in trouble my sweet mother would use her angry voice and call me Daniel Lynn. Any time I heard mom use my full legal name I knew she was upset, and I was in big trouble. I won't repeat the names my brothers called me when they were mad at me. Looking back it is no wonder I was confused as a junior high student. My identity kept changing, my name kept changing, and when I finally hit puberty several other things changed. Acne and hormones are enough to give any young man an identity crisis.

When I started my freshman year of high school in 1981, if you would have asked me who Dan Meers was, I would've told you he was a student and an athlete. At the same time, if you would have asked my fellow classmates they would have told you I was a class clown and benchwarmer, which was probably much closer to the truth. At this stage in my life, being accepted by my friends was very important to me. As a freshman, I would have done anything to be liked.

One of the reasons I struggled with my confidence when I entered high school was because too often I allowed my value to be determined by others. My identity and how I felt about myself were often dictated by what others said about me and the labels they placed on me. Needless to say, this was not a healthy way to live life; it only created more insecurity.

I discovered my identity during my senior year of high school. In 1985 I attended a Fellowship of Christian Athletes (FCA) Weekend of Champions event in Eureka, MO. FCA advertised it as a weekend filled with inspiration and perspiration, but what really got me to sign up was finding out there would be friends, food and fun. I saw this as a great chance to get away from home and spend an exciting weekend with my buddies.

What I didn't realize at the time was this FCA weekend conference would end up being a life-changing experience which continues to impact and define my life today. The weekend delivered everything it promised. I spent time with my buddies and even made some new friends with other high school students from the St. Louis area. We ate lots of food and had a whole lot of fun. Also just as promised, the weekend was filled with inspiration. On the final day of camp if you walked into our cabin you would quickly know our clothes were also filled with perspiration. However, what made the weekend one I will never forget was the change that took place in my heart.

As much as I hated to admit it, when I arrived at the FCA conference I was a very self-centered and prideful individual. On the outside I gave off the impression I was a pretty good guy, but deep down inside I knew I was really only concerned about three people–me, myself and I. English theologian John Owen once said, "Selfishness is the making a man's self his own centre, the beginning and end of all he doeth." At that time in my life this described Dan Meers perfectly. I was at the center, sitting on the throne of my own selfish little kingdom. I was living as if the world should revolve around me. When it didn't I would get upset. At this point, I hadn't learned the very important life lesson that selfish people are seldom happy people.

Throughout the weekend our conference speaker kept talking about having a personal relationship with Jesus. I was very familiar with this guy named Jesus because I had grown up going to church and had even attended a Christian elementary school. I almost always prayed before my meals, and occasionally I even tossed a few coins in the offering plate at church. At the time, I considered myself a religious person, but at the FCA weekend I discovered there was a big difference between being religious and having a relationship with Jesus.

Saturday evening as I sat listening to the speaker share about his personal relationship with Jesus, I knew he had something in his life I was missing. Even though I knew a lot about Jesus, I didn't really 'know' Jesus. It dawned on me I knew Jesus a lot like I knew Abraham Lincoln. I had read and heard stories about both men and had even seen pictures of both Jesus and Honest Abe. From everything I had learned at church and in school, both Jesus and President Lincoln seemed like great guys who did a lot of really nice things for others. Although I would never get the opportunity to have a relationship with Abraham Lincoln because he died in 1865, Jesus was different. Even though He also died, the speaker reminded us three days after His death on a cross, Jesus rose from the grave. Because He was alive, we could have a relationship with Him.

As I locked in to the speaker's words, I knew I had spent my life just going through the motions. My religion was nothing more than a boring routine. My religious practices weren't affecting the way I was living my life. Deep down I was an insecure, selfish and sinful young man who still thought he could somehow earn his way into heaven by trying to be good. Up to this point, I believed the lie that since I was a 'pretty good kid' who had never committed any of the big sins, God would somehow just let me slide into heaven. I had deceived myself into thinking that sins were weighted. There were big sins and little sins in this world. Since I had never committed any of those big bad sins, I somehow only needed a little bit of God's forgiveness.

The speaker shared how all men have one thing in common. We are all sinners in need of God's forgiveness. None of us can ever be good enough to earn salvation apart from Him. The Bible says, "God saved you by his grace when you believed. And you can't take credit for this; it is a gift from God. Salvation is not a reward for the good things we have done, so none of us can boast about it" (Ephesians 2:8-9, NLT).

He explained salvation is not something we can earn for ourselves. Instead it is a free gift God offers to us strictly because He loves us. Each of us has to choose whether to accept or reject God's free gift. The final Bible verse shared by the speaker caused me to pause and reflect. He said, "And this is the testimony: God has given us eternal life and this life is in His Son. Whoever has the Son has life; whoever does not have the Son of God does not have life" (1 John 5:11-12).

I knew the time had come for me to quit pretending and get my life right with God. I no longer wanted to be satisfied with just knowing about Jesus, I wanted Him in my life. If I really wanted my life to be different it was time to begin a personal relationship with the one who had died on a cross for my sins.

I knew I didn't have all the answers, and I wasn't exactly sure what a relationship with Jesus even looked like, but I knew the time had come to surrender my life to the one who had given His life for me. With tears in my eyes I prayed the most sincere prayer I had ever prayed. I asked God to forgive me for being a selfish, prideful and sinful man. I invited Jesus into my life and asked Him to help me turn from my sins and live a life pleasing to Him. I put my faith in His sacrificial death on the cross, rather than based on my own good works. Finally, I asked Him to be my new best friend and gave Him permission to mold and shape me into the man He had created me to be.

When I finished my prayer I didn't see any bright lights from heaven, and I didn't hear an audible voice from God saying, "Way to go Dan." However, what I did experience was a deep peace in my heart I had never experienced before. Some people call it being born again and others call it getting saved. I honestly didn't care what they called it. All I knew was something was different. At the time I couldn't explain it, but I knew I was a changed man.

Over the next several weeks as I read my Bible daily I discovered God makes hundreds of promises to those who love Him. One of the verses which helped me better understand what had happened in my life was 2 Corinthians 5:17, "Anyone who belongs to Christ has become a new person. The old life is gone; a new life has begun!"

As I began to grow in my newfound faith, I began discovering my true identity. The Bible became much more exciting to me. In the book of John it says, "But to all who believed him and accepted him, He gave the right to become children of God" (John 1:12, NLT). I began to understand my identity was never meant to be based on what I did, how I performed or upon the opinions of others. This is foolishness and only leads to a life filled with insecurities. I am a child of God. That is my true identity. No matter what happens to me in life this fact never changes. What others say about me isn't nearly as important as what God has to say about me. As I read God's Word each day I discover it isn't a big book filled with a list of do's and don'ts, it's actually God's love letter to me. The more I read, the more I discover my value and worth.

Psalm 119:13-14 says, "For you created my inmost being; you knit me together in my mother's womb. I praise you because I am fearfully and wonderfully made." I'm not some random, cosmic accident like my high school science book claimed. I didn't evolve from a bunch of monkeys, even though you might suspect it if you ever attend one of my family reunions and watch us eat. No, I am handmade, custom designed and fully loaded by God to do awesome things. I was created *by* God and *for* God, and my purpose in life is to serve Him. I know God has a plan for my life, and His plan is much greater than me living a self-centered life. I am created to be a difference maker in this world. Each of us is designed to be a difference maker who makes a positive impact in the lives of others.

Becoming Mission Minded: Your identity is tied directly to whatever you give your heart to. Ultimately your identity will be tied to what you love the most. What do you love the most? Is what you love the most going to last, or can it be taken away? And if and when it goes away, what will you be left with? Where do you find your identity and purpose? Is it based on what God says about you or on what others say?

18

Slap Me on the Butt, Jesus

"Life is too short to waste time on things that have no lasting significance." - TB Joshua

I once heard the well-known evangelist Billy Graham say when he got to heaven he wanted to hear God say, "Well done my good and faithful servant." I've always been a sports guy, so when I get to heaven I just want Jesus to slap me on the butt and say, "Atta Boy Dan."

I know I can never repay Him for my many blessings, but I can sure try to share my blessings with those around me by the way I choose to live. Every day in small ways, I have the opportunity with my words and through my actions to be a blessing to others in this world. I don't want my primary focus in this life to be on my own achievement, advancement or accumulation. Those things are nice, but if they become my primary focus my life will lack meaning and purpose. I don't want my motivation to come from accolades, awards or applause. I don't want to be motivated by feelings because my feelings are often selfish. I want my motivation to come from my love of God and my love for others.

In their book, *The Love Dare*, Stephen and Alex Kendrick said, "You need to understand that your heart always follows your investment." In other words, whatever you pour your time, talent and treasure into, your heart will follow. At the beginning of this book I mentioned three things in my life I am truly passionate about: my faith, my family and using my life to make a positive impact in this world. These are the areas in which I want to invest. During my time on this earth these are the three areas I want to give my heart. God has given me a crazy platform as a mascot to hopefully bring smiles to people's faces, but He has also put a fire in my belly to help those around me who are hurting and struggling in life.

As I travel around the world I meet many people who are lonely, neglected, forgotten and devalued. I believe we each have a responsibility to care for these people. We have a responsibility to help the widows, orphans, and the oppressed and hurting. If God cares deeply for these people, we need to do the same.

People can be hungry in many ways. They may have plenty of food to eat but are starving to feel valuable. The world is full of people suffering not only physically but also emotionally. This is often caused by abuse, rejection, abandonment, disappointment, criticism or negative behaviors by others. This emotional pain can be just as devastating as physical pain because people feel they have to hide it and pretend it isn't real.

The Bible says, "God gives a hand to those down on their luck, gives a fresh start to those ready to quit" (Psalm 145:14, MSG). How does He do this? He works through people. Ordinary people like you and me. He's looking for loving, committed and dedicated individuals who are willing to invest their lives to help meet the needs of others.

Mother Teresa once said, "Do not think that love, in order to be genuine, has to be extraordinary. What we need is to love without getting tired." Mother Teresa was a woman who invested her time and energy to help those less fortunate. Because of the love she demonstrated, she was able to make an incredible impact in the lives of others. The Bible says, "So let's not get tired of doing what is good. At just the right time we will reap a harvest of blessing if we don't give up. Therefore, whenever we have the opportunity, we should do good to everyone..." (Galatians 6:9, NLT). Mother Teresa lived out this verse as well as anyone I know. I hope the same can be said of my life someday.

As I mentioned in Chapter 1, I'm not as young as I used to be. There are many things in my life now that point to the fact I'm getting older. Recently I caught myself turning out the lights at home for economic rather than romantic reasons. When I get off work, I look forward to a dull evening at home rather than a wild night out on the town. When Cam and I go out to eat at a nice restaurant with dimmed lights and ambiance, I have to use the flashlight on my cell phone to read the menu. Things have definitely changed. As much as I try to fight it, Father Time is catching up to me.

My good friend Rod Handley likes to say, "We are all like a jug of milk; we all come with an expiration date. The only difference is that our expiration date is not printed on us." I love his quote because it reminds me I have a limited number of days here on this earth.

I don't know when my expiration date will be, but I do know every day God gives me between today and whenever my expiration date arrives, I want to live this life to the fullest. I believe we were designed by God to conquer, not to cower. I believe my life's purpose is bigger than simply playing out my own dream. I want to be a part of God's bigger story. I don't want to be lured into a life of selfishness and indifference. If life is all about me, I will never become the kind of husband, father and man God designed me to be. I'll do things with the wrong self-focused motives. This is not how I want to live. I want to use every day I get to be a blessing in the lives of others. I want my life to build up others, starting in my own home and then spreading into my workplace, community and world.

If I want my life to make a difference in the lives of others, then it starts with my choices. Life is made of choices. Choices will either make or break a person. They have the potential to cause much joy or regret. They can be a person's greatest asset or their greatest liability. I want my personal choices to always reflect my love for God and my love for others.

Therefore, if I want to be a difference maker in this world I need to hang around like minded people. The friends with whom we surround ourselves will either influence us in a positive way or infect us in a negative way. I'm thankful God has placed so many passionate and purposeful people in my life. I've mentioned many of these people in this book. Hanging around friends who are passionate and know who they are, and why they are, has encouraged me to do the same. They have encouraged me on my journey and have been a huge blessing in my life.

For the past three decades I've had the privilege of speaking to hundreds of thousands of people all across the country at schools, churches, corporations, banquets and conferences. My goal as a speaker is to challenge people to action. I try to encourage them to get off the sidelines and get involved in the game. Life is much more rewarding and exciting when you live as a participant instead of a spectator.

Don't be afraid to get dirty and get a few bruises. Leave it all on the field. In other words, give life everything you've got. Don't settle for making a living. Make a life. Don't just take a job for the paycheck. Go after a career which lines up with the passions God has placed deep in your heart.

I often tell my audiences, halfway is no way to live life, you've got to go all in. My goal as an author is very similar. I hope this book has challenged you to develop a love for life and not settle for status or status quo. Although I certainly hope you have enjoyed reading this book, enjoyment was not my primary purpose for writing it. The main reason I wrote this book was to challenge you to get out of your comfort zone, get involved and make a positive difference in the lives of others in your little corner of the world.

I hope the words in this book touch you in two places. First, I hope my words have touched your heart. I hope you have been reminded that you are valuable because of who you are, not because of what you do. You were created by God and for God. That's your true identity. God never makes mistakes or junk. We are all hand-made, custom-designed, and fully loaded by God to do awesome things.

Unfortunately, I believe there is an epidemic of insecurity which is stealing the joy of life from many people. I know first-hand the effect of insecurity on people's lives because I have experienced it myself. Those who are insecure often seek the approval of others to try to overcome feelings of rejection and low self-esteem. They become approval addicts. When struggling with insecurity, only one thing will set us free, and that is God's truth.

The truth is we don't need to struggle to get from man what God freely gives us: love, acceptance, approval, security, worth and value. Our worth, value and acceptance come from Him. As long as we have those, we have the most valuable things in the world. I hope this truth touches your heart and transforms your life.

You know where else I hope my words touched you? When you finish reading this book, I also hope you feel like I lovingly kicked you in the rear end. If you read this book and commit to doing even one little thing to be a blessing in someone else's life, then all the hours I spent writing will have been worth it. I hope you decide to join in on the action and begin living a life of influence.

In March 2017 I attended one of the most encouraging funerals of my life. It was truly a celebration of a life lived well. The funeral was for my friend Dan Erickson, who had passed away after a hard-fought battle against ALS, also known as Lou Gehrig's disease.

I met Dan at church shortly after Cam and I moved into our first home in Lee's Summit. I loved spending time with Dan because he was a man who loved life. Do you know anybody like that? People like Dan are contagious. They are fun to be around. They are difference makers. I loved spending time with Dan because nobody loved life more than he did, and nobody loved people more than my friend Dan.

I once heard him say that his biggest fear in life was not failure. His biggest fear was succeeding in life at things that don't really matter. The more I think about Dan's quote the more I love it. I respected Dan because of the way he lived his life. That day, as I sat with hundreds of other people at his funeral, it was obvious Dan was loved by many. He impacted many lives during his time on this earth. Dan lived out a very important life lesson we all need to remember. He understood it's nice to have things that money can buy, but in the long run it's even better to have those things in this life that money can't buy. Even though Dan didn't have a large bank account, he was one of the richest men I knew.

When Dan got to the end of his life, his body was used up. ALS had taken its toll. Even though his body was weak though, Dan was still at peace. For years he had been living his life for the things that truly mattered. He had been writing a life story he could be proud of. Dan left a legacy because of the choices he made each and every day. He chose to invest his days on this earth wisely. Because of this mindset, he had written a life story his family and friends could celebrate. On the bottom of the program I received at Dan's funeral it read,

"Live your life with No Regrets, No Retreats and No Reserves." - Dan Erickson

This sums up how I want to live. I hope to live my life the way Dan lived his, by loving God and loving people. I refuse to live my life focused on myself. Instead I want to live with my eyes open, looking for opportunities to help those who are hurting. I don't want to get to the end of my life and look back with regrets. I don't want to look back someday and discover I wasted my time on this earth on things which didn't really matter. I want to leave a godly legacy, one that impacts and influences the lives of others. What about you? What kind of legacy would you like to leave behind? How do you hope to be remembered at your funeral?

I promise your greatest legacy won't be the material things you leave behind. Those will all fade away. Your greatest legacy will be the love you leave behind. This is the legacy which endures. It will endure in the lives of your children and in the lives of others your life has touched. I hope to one day be remembered not only as a Mascot on a Mission but more importantly as a Man on a Mission who invested his time, treasures and talents to make this world a better place. A man who loved God, loved others and lived a life of influence.

Becoming Mission Minded: Are you living your life on mission? Are you living a life of influence? It's never too late to start. Has this book lovingly kicked you in the rear and challenged you to become a man (or woman) on a mission? If so, please share your story and this book with someone else.

My Favorite Quotes on Life, Love, Laughter & Leadership

"Life is like a coin; you can spend it any way you wish, but you can only spend it once, so spend wisely."

"God didn't put us on this earth to make a living. He put us here to make an impact."

"Don't settle for being merely a teller of stories about significance. Decide to be the story of significance. Become the central character in your story of making a difference!" - John C. Maxwell

"This is the beginning of a brand new day. God has given me this day to use as I will. I can waste it or I can use it for good, but what I do today is important because I'm exchanging a day of my life for it. When tomorrow comes this day is going to be gone forever, leaving in its place something I have traded for it. I want it to be gain and not loss, good and not evil, success and not failure, in order that I shall not regret the price I have paid for it." – Dr. Heartsill Wilson

"When you intentionally use your everyday life to bring about positive change in the lives of others, you begin to live a life that matters." - John C. Maxwell

"In seeking happiness for others, you find it for yourself."

"Life is not about any particular achievement or experience. The most important task of your life is not what you do, but who you become."

"A random act of kindness, no matter how small, can make a tremendous impact on someone else's life." - Roy T. Bennett

"I am a little pencil in the hand of a writing God who is sending a love letter to the world." - Mother Teresa

"It's nice to be important, but it's more important to be nice." - John Templeton

"To put significance in our stories, we must also take action. Being passive may feel safe. If you do nothing, nothing can go wrong. But while inaction cannot fail, it cannot succeed either. We can wait, and hope, and wish, but if we do, we miss the stories our lives could be." - John C. Maxwell

"This life is for loving, sharing, learning, smiling, caring, forgiving, laughing, hugging, helping, dancing, wondering, healing, and even more loving. I choose to live life this way. I want to live my life in such a way that when I get out of bed in the morning, the devil says, 'aw sh*t, he's up!" - Steve Maraboli

"To make a difference in someone's life you don't have to be brilliant, rich, beautiful, or perfect. You just have to care enough and be there."

"In this life we cannot always do great things. But we can do small things with great love." - Mother Teresa

"No one is useless in this world who lightens the burdens of another." - Charles Dickens

"The urgent things in life are seldom important, and the important things in life are seldom urgent."

"And don't forget to do good and share with those in need. These are the sacrifices that please God" (Hebrews 13:16, NLT).

"Do your little bit of good where you are; it's those little bits of good put together that overwhelm the world."
- Desmond Tutu

"It's only after you've stepped outside your comfort zone that you begin to change, grow and transform." - Roy T. Bennett

"Great leaders don't set out to be a leader, they set out to make a difference. It's never about the role, always about the goal." - Jeremy Bravo

"Be decisive. Right or wrong, make a decision. The road of life is paved with flat squirrels who couldn't make a decision."

"Success is not how high you have climbed, but how you make a positive difference to the world." - Roy T. Bennett

"Never underestimate the valuable and important difference you make in every life you touch, for the impact you make today has a powerful rippling effect on every tomorrow."
- Leon Brown

"Our greatest wealth is not measured in terms of riches but relationships."

"We can change the world and make it a better place. It is in our hands to make a difference." - Nelson Mandela

Every morning you wake up, everyone has something to complain about and everyone has something to be thankful for. Whichever one you choose to focus on will determine your attitude for the day.

"Stop acting as if life is a rehearsal. Live this day as if it were your last. The past is over and gone. The future is not guaranteed." - Wayne Dyer

"Scars show us where we have been; they do not dictate where we are going." - David Rossi

"It's not how far you fall, but how high you bounce that counts." - Zig Ziglar

"Our job is to love others without stopping to inquire whether or not they are worthy."

"Don't wait for other people to be loving, giving, compassionate, grateful, forgiving, generous, or friendly...lead the way!"

"No one has ever become poor by giving." - Anne Frank

"I want to be givin' while I'm livin' so I'm knowin' where it's goin.'"

"Your walk talks and your talk talks, but your walk talks louder than your talk talks."

"Be the reason someone smiles. Be the reason someone feels loved and believes in the goodness of people." - Roy T. Bennett

"In life you get what you put in. When you make a positive impact in someone else's life, you also make a positive impact in your own life."

"If you wish to make a positive impact in the world, you must separate yourself from the crowd."

"You can never have an impact on society if you have not changed yourself." - Nelson Mandela

"Don't use social media to impress people; use it to impact people." - Dave Willis

"We love others best when we love God most."

"Without God, life has no purpose and without purpose life has no meaning. Without meaning, life has no significance or hope." - Rick Warren

"Let your light shine before men in such a way that they may see your good works and glorify your Father who is in heaven" (Matthew 5:16, NASB).

Optimist Creed

Promise Yourself ...

- To be so strong that nothing can disturb your peace of mind.
- To talk health, happiness and prosperity to every person you meet.
- To make all your friends feel that there is something in them.
- To look at the sunny side of everything and make your optimism come true.
- To think only of the best, to work only for the best, and to expect only the best.
- To be just as enthusiastic about the success of others as you are about your own.
- To forget the mistakes of the past and press on to the greater achievements of the future.
- To wear a cheerful countenance at all times and give every living creature you meet a smile.
- To give so much time to the improvement of yourself that you have no time to criticize others.
- To be too large for worry, too noble for anger, too strong for fear, and too happy to permit the presence of trouble.

"Don't worry what you could do if you lived your life over; get busy with what's left."

Acknowledgements

Writing a book is like working as an NFL mascot. From the outside it may appear glamorous, but when you're the guy dancing around inside a hot, furry costume it's a lot of hard work. This book was written on airplanes, in hotel rooms and almost every room of my home. Several times I woke up in the middle of the night, got out of bed and jotted down my thoughts because I knew if I waited until morning, I would forget them. Mascots have to take advantage of those brief moments of inspiration because they don't come along very often. I spent many frustrating days sitting and staring at my computer, trying to figure out the best way to express myself, so writing this book is very similar to performing as KC Wolf at Chiefs games. There are times of great excitement, moments of tremendous frustration, and by the end of the fourth quarter you're just thankful it's finally over. Winston Churchhill once said, "Writing a book is an adventure to begin with; it is a toy and an amusement, then it becomes a mistress, and then it becomes a master, and then a tyrant. The last phase is that just as you are about to be reconciled to your servitude, you kill the monster and fling him out to the public." Churchhill's words ring true as I feel as though I'm flinging this monster out to the world!

There are many people in my life who helped make this book become a reality. Like every other accomplishment in my life I have a lot of wonderful people to thank:

Cam: Our medicine cabinet used to be filled with Flintstone chewable vitamins, but now we've moved on to Centrum Silver and Metamucil. I can't imagine sharing this journey with anybody else. I'm looking forward to living happily ever after with you until death do us part. I LOVE YOU!!! xxooxxooXXooXx

Mycah, Aaron, and Mallory: You made it through the teenage years, and I've still got most of my hair. Thanks for being awesome kids. Other men may think their children are the best, but that's because they never got the privilege of being your dad. I love you, and I'm very proud of each of you. Keep living by Faith and not Fear because I know God has great plans for each of you (Jeremiah 29:11).

Kyndal and Brendan: You are both an answer to my prayers. I didn't get to choose who my kids would marry, but I couldn't be happier with the choices they made. I love being your father-in-law. I'm thankful I gained a bonus son and daughter without having to pay for your college. I love you both

Rusty: Your constant licking made it challenging to concentrate on writing this book. You leave hair on my carpet and you crap in my yard, but overall, you're a pretty good dog. Thanks for keeping me company during my late-night writing sessions.

Mom and Dad: I've met a lot of cheerleaders during my career, and though they may be cuter, none of them cheered for me as loudly as you did. Thanks for all the love, support and encouragement through the years. I couldn't have asked for a better set of role models. I love you both very much!

Jim and Nancy: Thanks for letting this dumb jock marry your beautiful daughter. I know everybody else in the family has a master's degree, but thank you for accepting me and my BS (That's Bachelor of Science by the way)!

Honey, Dave and Stacey, Tom and Kerry, Jim and Kristen, nieces, nephews, in-laws, out-laws, cousins, aunts, uncles and everyone else related to me: You weren't much help writing this book, but I included your names anyway. Don't forget my birthday is on January 7, and gift cards work just fine. I love you all!

The Hunt family: I can't begin to tell you how grateful I am that you've allowed me to represent the Kansas City Chiefs for the past three decades as your #1 fan, KC Wolf. Your commitment to excellence both on the field and in the community are inspiring. I'm thankful to work for an organization that not only preaches the importance of giving back but also puts it into practice. Thanks for allowing me to use my platform as an NFL mascot to positively impact others not only in Kansas City but around the world.

My Kansas City Chiefs co-workers: I not only have the greatest job in the world, but I also work with the greatest people in the world. Thanks for your friendship and for putting up with the Director of Shenanigans, even when I arrive at work smelling 'less than fresh.'

Chiefs Kingdom: You truly are the greatest fans any mascot could hope for. When I began as KC Wolf I was just a young pup, and now I'm slowly turning into an old dog. Through the years you've invited me to join your birthdays, weddings, marriage proposals and even baby gender reveals. Thanks for the countless smiles you've brought to my face and the joy you've added to my life.

Bobby Bell: You're an NFL Hall of Famer in more ways than one, my friend. Thanks for the influence your life has had on so many, including me.

Mike DeBacker, Rod Handley, William Hanna, Fred Olson and Bruce Rehmer: Thank you for holding me accountable each week and challenging me to be the husband, father, friend and man God designed me to be. Thanks also for the positive influence you've had on me and my family. I'm grateful for all the pats on the back and the kicks in the butt which have helped to keep me on the straight and narrow. I love you guys!

Gordon Thiessen: You remind me of Clark Kent. A superhero in civilian clothes. Thanks for all you did to help make this book a reality.

Alan Goforth, Ty Hester, Don Hilkemeier, Andrew Mather, Dan Smith and Michelle Montgomery Trazzera: Thank you for your assistance with proofreading and pictures. Your honest feedback and advice were extremely helpful. Thanks most of all for your friendship!

Laura Maxwell: You're amazing. Thanks for paying more attention in your English classes than I ever did. Your book editing skills help me look a lot more intelligent.

My KC Wolf backups (past and present) Jon Kindler, Andrew Johnson, Shawn Emerson, Ky Turner, Brady Testorff, Jordan Bunce, Adrian Iliescu, Wade Shapp, Drake Fenlon, Moses Weiss, Kyle Rock and Derek Handley: You guys make me feel like a proud father. Thanks for being part the Wolf family and for the impact you have had on so many lives in our community. I've seen you at your best, and I've smelled you at your worst. I appreciate you guys and all your hard work. I'm grateful for the laughs you've brought to my life!

My NFL Furternity brothers: You guys are a bunch of animals in more ways than one. They say you can't teach an old dog new tricks, but I would disagree. You continue to teach me not only how to be a better mascot but more importantly how to be a better man. I love you knuckleheads!

My Lord and Savior Jesus Christ: The only reason my life can influence others is because your life has impacted me. Thank you that my identity is no longer found in what I do or what others say, but my true identity is found in You. Thanks for adopting me into your family and allowing this wolf to become one of your sheep. I'm forever grateful that you have filled my heart with joy and given me a purpose to live for (Psalm 16:11).

Get In The Game

Are you looking for a way to make a difference in the lives of others? Here are some great organizations making an impact close to home and around the world. Pick a cause you're passionate about and get involved:

- City Union Mission–Kansas City, MO
  www.cityunionmission.org
- Compassion International–Colorado Springs, CO
  www.compassion.com
- Convoy of Hope–Springfield, MO
  www.convoyofhope.org
- Global Orphan Project–Kansas City, MO
  www.goproject.org
- Grace Mission–Henderson, NE
  www.gracemission.info
- Hopegivers International–Columbus, GA
  www.hopegivers.org
- Hope House–Lee's Summit, MO
  www.hopehouse.net
- Joy Meadows–Basehor, KS
  www.joymeadows.org
- Miracle Foundation–Austin, TX
  www.miraclefoundation.org
- Prison Fellowship–Merrifield, VA
  www.prisonfellowship.org
- Rachel House–Lee's Summit, MO
  www.rachelhouse.org
- Reliant Ministries–Orlando, FL
  www.reliant.org
- Restoration House–Kansas City, MO
  www.restorationhousekc.com

- Shelter KC (formerly KCRM)–Kansas City, MO
  www.shelterkc.org
- Tim Tebow Foundation–Jacksonville, FL
  www.timtebowfoundation.org
- Topeka Rescue Mission–Topeka, KS
  www.trmonline.org
- World Vision–Federal Way, WA
  www.worldvision.org

About the Author

Dan Meers goes to work each day like many other men, dressed in a suit. The only difference is that instead of wearing a tie with his suit, Dan wears a tail. You see, Dan is a professional mascot.

Dan began his career in 1986 at the University of Missouri-Columbia. Dressed as the school mascot, Truman Tiger, it didn't take long for Dan to establish himself as one of the top college mascots in the nation. After finishing second in 1988, Dan was selected the nation's #1 college mascot at the 1989 National Collegiate Mascot Championships. As graduation approached, Dan began to receive offers to use his talents at the professional level. After graduating with honors, Dan decided to trade in his tiger stripes for bird feathers and began his professional career as Fredbird, the mascot for the St. Louis Cardinals baseball team. Although many thought Dan's "bird legs" were a perfect match for his costume in St. Louis, Dan stayed only a short time. He was offered a job in professional football and decided to exchange his bird suit to become a wolf.

Today Dan is widely known as KC Wolf, the official mascot of the Kansas City Chiefs. He travels throughout the United States and the world, entertaining thousands of people both in and out of costume. Dan is in high demand not only as a mascot but also as a humorous and motivational speaker to audiences of all ages. His enthusiasm, optimism and love for life are contagious and make Dan an inspiration to all those he meets.

After listening to Dan, you realize what makes him so truly special is his genuine desire to motivate others to enjoy life as much as he does. The constant smile he wears comes from within. The humorous message he shares has encouraged thousands to strive for the best in life and enjoy it each and every step along the way.

If you are interested in having Dan Meers speak to your organization, church, school or ministry please contact him at: **dmeers@chiefs.nfl.com** or **www.characterthatcounts.org**

Follow KC Wolf on Facebook at KC Wolf
on Twitter@KCWOLF
or at: www.kcchiefs.com/cheerleaders/kc-wolf.html or at
www.DanMeers.org

NOTE ON BOOK PROCEEDS

All net proceeds and royalties from the sale of this book and my first book *Wolves Can't Fly* are used to fund missions and ministries aiding orphans and the poor around the world through the 501(c)(3) ministry of Character That Counts. A special thanks to over 500 organizations (schools, corporations, state/county/city agencies, churches and ministries) who have purchased books after speaking engagements all across the nation. Through March 2023, more than $220,000 has been given, and we can't wait to give even more away in future years. See www.characterthatcounts.org for more information.

"Religion that God our Father accepts as pure and faultless is this: to look after orphans and widows in their distress and to keep oneself from being polluted by the world" (James 1:27).

Ordering Wolves Can't Fly

You can order more books from the author at www.danmeers.org or the publisher at www.crosstrainingpublishing.com.

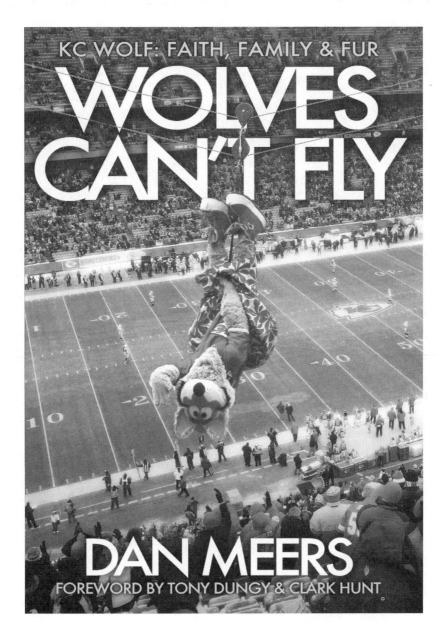